Yukon Gold

Dedicated to the memory of the men and women who, armed with indomitable courage and spirit, breached the Canadian frontier.

Yukon Gold

High Hopes and Dashed Dreams

by

James Preyde and Susan Preyde

hancock

house

ISBN 0-88839-362-8
Copyright © 1995 James Preyde and Susan Preyde

Cataloging in Publication Data
Preyde, James, 1957–
   Yukon gold
   High hopes and dashed dreams

   ISBN 0-88839-362-8

   1. Klondike River Valley (Yukon)—Gold discoveries.
2. Yukon Territory—History—1895–1918.* I. Preyde,
Susan, 1957– II. Title.
FC4022.3.P73 1995   971.9'102   C95-910148-9
F1095.K5P73 1995

Edited: Suzanne Chin
Production: Myron Shutty
Cover photo: National Archives of Canada

Published simultaneously in Canada and the United States by

HANCOCK HOUSE PUBLISHERS LTD.
19313 Zero Avenue, Surrey, B.C. V4P 1M7
(604) 538-1114   Fax (604) 538-2262

HANCOCK HOUSE PUBLISHERS
1431 Harrison Avenue, Blaine, WA 98230-5005
(604) 538-1114   Fax (604) 538-2262

Contents

Preface

One of Canada's great stories is that of the Klondike Gold Rush. When news of gold struck the cash-strapped economically depressed world of the 1890s, Canada was suddenly the place to be.

Imagine the desperation that ripped men and women from the comforts of hearth and home and drove them into the frozen feral hinterland. What yearning possessed them, giving them the strength to surmount the barriers of a hostile land and all the fury that nature could unleash? Picture the isolation and despair when all was lost and, thousands of miles from home, they resigned themselves to failure.

Yukon Gold: High Hopes and Dashed Dreams looks at the invincible human spirit in the context of one of Canada's most important historical events. Sir Wilfred Laurier predicted that the twentieth century would be Canada's century. During the Klondike Gold Rush, it looked as though that would be true.

1

The Prolific Rabbit

In the summer of 1896 the marshy flat at the confluence of the Klondike and Yukon rivers was sporadically visited by trappers and surveyors. Their visits were short, the vicinity a stopover on the way to a more significant location. The following summer, the site was covered with a multitude of tents and quickly built buildings. By the summer of 1898, the same location was atop the most valuable piece of real estate in the world and Dawson was in its heyday.

Most citizens of adolescent Canada had little knowledge of the Arctic's districts. Unseen by white men prior to the 1820s, these areas were largely unexplored, ill defined and inhospitable. In 1896 the Yukon was a district of the Northwest Territories with little more than the occasional supply post dotting its landscape but abundant mineral treasures lay waiting for the mass exploitation that would put the Yukon on the world's map and change its face forever.

There is some debate as to the identity of the first white man to visit the Yukon. Sir John Franklin reached Herschel Island in 1825 while looking for the *Northwest Passage* and was surprised to find the Inuit armed with metal-tipped arrowheads which, they explained, were received in trade from white men to the west. This led Franklin to the assumption that these white men must be trappers from the Russian American Company, which was established in 1799 to place all Russian possessions in North America under a corporation.[1] It would seem likely that Russian visits to the Yukon predated Franklin by at least twenty-five years.

Robert Campbell of the Hudson's Bay Company has also been described as the first white man in the Yukon Territory, visiting the Frances Lake area in 1842.[2] The name *Yukon,* a native word meaning great river, was first applied by John Bell of the Hudson's Bay Company in 1846.[3] John Bell was a chief trader with the Hudson's Bay Company in the 1830s and 1840s. He is widely believed to be the first white man to reach the Yukon River from the Mackenzie.[4]

In the early part of the nineteenth century much of the vast north was a land grant to the Hudson's Bay Company. The company's quest for lucrative furs was leading it farther west from its old stomping grounds around Hudson Bay. As trade and commerce increased, the Hudson's Bay Company had a desire to establish a route to the Pacific and gave Robert Campbell, a young, ambitious and tireless Scot who was apprenticed to the company, the responsibility of exploring the western Arctic in the 1830s. Campbell brought with him the Hudson's Bay Company's official policy of dealing with natives; friendly yet cautious, unnecessary use of firearms was discouraged and weapons were kept out of sight if at all possible. Sometimes this did not work, as when confrontation erupted with the Nahannis in 1839. The Nahannis were a tribe inhabiting the Dease and Liard river areas who had been trading with the Russian American Company. The Russian American Company had been rather generous in trade, trading at up to ten times the value of goods offered by the Hudson's Bay Company. The Nahannis expected equal treatment from the

8

Hudson's Bay Company, and when their demands were not met, the Nahannis robbed the traders and tried to push the Hudson's Bay Company out of the area.[5] But usually there was a more harmonious relationship in the early meetings between the two cultures. Outward appearances might indicate a humanitarian inclination, but the Hudson's Bay Company was a profit-motivated organization and the Indian was a valuable asset, a skilled hunter and proficient guide. In return the natives got the usual trinkets and baubles along with liquor and exotic foreign diseases from Europe.

The natives developed a fiercely competitive nature, striving to outdo their neighbors in the number of pelts produced. The trust the Hudson's Bay Company had attempted to instill in the natives quickly degenerated into dependence as the company's forts and trading posts became more established. The exploitation of the Yukon's first peoples intensified, consequently the natives were compelled to extend a desperate welcome to the rapidly-growing number of whites invading their homeland. This was in sharp contrast to the often bloody conflicts that occurred in the United States, such as Wounded Knee, and Little Big Horn.

The first notable gold find in the Yukon Valley occurred in 1863 when a small sample of the precious metal was sent to England by Reverend R. M. McDonald,[6] but it was apparently only a trace amount so did not attract much attention. A more substantial strike occurred in the Dease Lake vicinity in 1873 and with that the interest in trapping began to evolve into an interest in prospecting. People slowly began trekking into the area, keeping an eye on the streams and an ear to the ground.

Most serious gold miners remained preoccupied with the San Francisco Rush of 1849 or the more recent rush in Barkerville, British Columbia, in the late 1860s. Those who had not become rich there had moved on to other parts of the country, the continent, or the world, bent on making their dreams come true. As good a place as any for some of them was the Yukon.

The facts of the actual discovery that sparked the Klondike Gold Rush are clouded by time. In August, 1896, George Carmack and two native fishing buddies, *Skookum Jim* and *Tagish Charley* were exploring in the area of the Klondike River. Carmack, from California, was married to Skookum Jim's sister, Kate. Some accounts of the day place Kate among their number as well as Gracey, Carmack's daughter.[7]

Carmack and his companions encountered Bob Henderson, a prospector from Nova Scotia who had been exploring the area. Henderson suggested Carmack stake a claim near Henderson's camp, but was opposed to Carmack's native friends doing the same. Henderson made a racial slur which was overheard by Carmack's companions and discussed among the little group as they left Henderson behind. The group picked along a few of the creeks before meeting up again at Henderson's camp. A discussion of the prospects on Rabbit Creek followed, though exactly who initiated it remains steeped in controversy. Regardless, on the evening of August 16, Rabbit Creek did not disappoint. One version is that Carmack plucked a nugget from the edge of the creek bed; another, that Skookum Jim and Tagish Charley discovered gold in the creek while washing a pan.[8] That nugget of shiny gold sparked the world's greatest gold rush.

The next morning Carmack staked the claim and the group left to register the claim at *Fortymile*, a community about a day's sail away on the Yukon River. Though Carmack had promised Henderson he would send word back if he found anything of substance, he did not and Henderson's earlier slight of Carmack's native companions has been cited as the reason.[9] At Fortymile, Carmack registered three claims on the stream, one for himself, one for Tagish Charley and one for Skookum Jim.

Few old-timers believed the claims of gold to be found on Rabbit Creek, a seemingly unlikely spot and Carmack had a reputation for a vivid imagination.[10] However some men were unwilling to pass up even the most remote possibility and headed upstream towards the Klondike. As more and more did so, others quickly became caught up in the excitement. Prospectors arrived on Rabbit Creek and confirmed the find, quickly spreading word of the strike throughout the surrounding area. Rabbit Creek's name was changed to *Bonanza Creek* in honor of its precious condition. Within days the opulent little creek was staked from end to end by hopeful prospectors. The Eldorado Creek, a tributary of the Bonanza, was staked solid shortly thereafter. The hapless Bob Henderson toiled away fruitlessly on creeks just over the ridge, unaware of the raucous activity going on a few miles away. The Canadian government would later pension Henderson for his role in the Klondike Gold Rush.[11]

Activity on the Bonanza and Eldorado creeks soared as news of the discovery of August 16, 1896 overran the district. The miners set about harvesting the easy gold; the nuggets that lay in the stream beds or those unearthed after rudimentary digging and panning. As winter approached, the region's rivers quickly froze solid. Since the rivers were the easiest way to travel in the Yukon, few chose to venture into the bleak hinterland after freeze-up so the miners settled into a winter of making money hand over fist. With only the barest necessities available to purchase with their nuggets and gold dust, these hardy pioneers quickly grew rich.

William Ogilvie, a Canadian government surveyor, tried to get word of the developments to Ottawa but a preliminary report in the fall of 1896 was ignored. In January, Ogilvie followed up with another note reporting that the discoveries in the Klondike might have far-reaching consequences. Again this failed to spark interest. By the time a third note, dated mid-June reached Ottawa, the developments in the Klondike had already been relayed around the world; it was old news.[12]

As the miners ripped into their claims, Joseph Ladue, a Yukon trader who had run a supply post in the area, had a vision. He established a simple saw mill a few miles west of the creeks where the Klondike River flows into the Yukon. There, he began building wooden houses as fast as his little mill could spit out the lumber in anticipation of a raging real estate market.[13] The new town was named Dawson after his friend *Dr. George Mercer Dawson*. Dr. Dawson, a native of Pictou, Nova Scotia, was a well-regarded scientist and explorer who had been the director of the Geological Survey of Canada in 1895, and who had done an extensive survey of the Klondike-Yukon area in 1887.[14]

By April, 1897 Dawson's population was 1,500.[15] As the spring thaw began to reopen the rivers, the town's accumulated wealth was packed up to be shipped off to the south via the Yukon River. That summer, two steamships departed from Dawson City with three tons of gold on board.[16]

In the depressed economy of the late 1890s, news of three tons of gold was just the jolt the world needed. The stories of Yukon gold spread like wildfire. "As much gold as you could carry!", "All you had to do was bend over and pick it up!" The excitement of traveling to the uncharted Arctic alone lured many of those bitten by the wanderlust. The wild west days of gunslingers and cattle rustlers were being tamed by businessmen and clerks. The old cowpokes with fond memories of the *good old days* saw this as their chance to leave the popular sideshows and circuses and relive the action of their youth and it seemed everyone wanted a piece of the action. Carpenters dropped their hammers, surgeons dropped their scalpels, tailors dropped their pants and husbands left home promising speedy returns with unimaginable wealth.

Partnerships were organized to pool finances and sponsor one or two members for the trip north. Hands rubbing gleefully and, dollar signs dancing in their eyes, the partners would bid their stalwart trekkers a safe and speedy return so they could share in countless riches. Another custom similar to these partnerships was the practice of *grubstaking*—lending money to successful or experienced prospectors in return for a percentage; usually half of everything mined. Joseph Ladue had promised Bob Henderson a grubstake which was why Henderson had been so diligently prospecting the district.[17]

The four corners of the world were hearing of Canada's Klondike. Great scores of people began to converge on the towns of North America's west coast. Crafty entrepreneurial shopkeepers in these towns advertised arctic outfits selling everything one could need to endure the rigors of the bitter northern climate. Some were con artists who knew little or nothing about even the basic needs of survival in these frigid wilds.

All manner of maritime craft in varying degrees of seaworthiness were drafted into service to transport the throngs up the west coast to Alaska. From Alaska's panhandle prospectors could choose one of two routes over the Coast Mountains to the headwaters of the Yukon River and from there make their way downstream to Dawson. Those with more money and time often chose the route upriver from St. Michael on the west coast of Alaska. Either way, the men and women in the ragtag armada plying its way up the treacherous Pacific rim were experiencing the first leg of a perilous journey to the North.

The stampede was on.

2

What a Rush!

The trip up the west coast of North America in the late summer of 1897 was as hazardous as it was breathtaking. From a ship's starboard side the lush carpet of evergreen formed the base for the towering Coast Mountains. On the port side the Pacific Ocean alternately lashed and caressed the ships, according to the whim of nature. Even the relative shelter of the Inside Passage could not provide refuge from the storms and tempests generated in the vast Pacific.

Those vessels that didn't come to grief in the sea terminated their voyage at either Dyea or Skagway, communities a few miles apart on inlets at the head of the Lynn Canal on the Alaskan Panhandle. From Dyea the stampeders embarked on their trek over the famed Chilkoot Pass over sixteen miles away. From Skagway the would-be gold prospectors assaulted the White Pass.

Men and women attempting either route were hoping to reach Lake Bennett, British Columbia where they could build boats and continue their journey to the Klondike gold fields via the Yukon River; a voyage of some 500 miles.

Dyea had been the site of a Healy and Wilson trading post as well as a home base for native packers. With the advent of the Klondike Gold Rush, the population of the small camp grew quickly. People assailed Dyea's beaches day and night, often jumping from their ships into chest deep, frigid water to carry their packs to land. The 7,500 foot wharf was not completed until May, 1898, a few months after the major onslaught of stampeders.

Streets were laid out in a sensible pattern but any appearance of order ended there. Buildings and tents were erected with careless abandon and roads were often littered with packs and gear as their owners scurried about buying up provisions for the journey. Packers and prospective customers haggled over fees.

Gamblers, hotel owners, liquor store keepers and prostitutes set up shop to entertain new arrivals while panhandlers and pickpockets also plied their trade. Law and order was piecemeal and generally administered by the inhabitants of the town. *Miner's justice*, as it was called, was dispensed by the town's citizens in the early days in the absence of U.S. Marshals or duly-elected judges in those far reaches of the American frontier. In the interest of bringing some level of control to the situation, the miners themselves would sit in judgment of the accused culprit. These 'magistrates' were generally influenced, if not intimidated, by the atmosphere of the assembly. Stealing was the most common crime and punishment for theft was severe, with penalties ranging from orders for restitution to the dreaded *banishment*. On February 15, 1898, at Sheep Camp on the Chilkoot Trail, a man was stripped and lashed 15 times for theft.[1] Expulsion into the ruthless Alaskan wilderness spelled certain death. While the sentences may seem unduly harsh, it must be understood that stealing someone else's supplies had very grave implications in the far north where replacements, if they were available at all, were exceptionally expensive. The arrival of a legitimate judicial body into the Alaskan Panhandle brought a sigh of relief from just about everyone, accusers and accused alike.

15

Some gold seekers never made it farther than Dyea. Stories circulated through town about the hardships to be experienced farther along the trail, along with rumors that the gold fields were already staked. Disenchanted and disillusioned, they returned south on the near-empty boats, often without a penny to their names. They'd had quite enough adventure for one lifetime.

Today, Dyea is a ghost town marked only by the faint traces of a few roads, a few piles of lumber (former buildings slowly being reclaimed by mother nature), the ruins of the wharf and a notice board describing Dyea's heyday and decline. From a population peak of about 8,000 in 1897, Dyea's inhabitants numbered just one by 1903; Emil Klatt, a vegetable farmer, busied himself picking among the ruins of the boom-bust town.[2] With the obvious decline by late 1898, many buildings were dismantled and the lumber sold in Skagway, or removed to Washington and Oregon states to be used in towns with a future.

The Chilkoot Trail is thirty-three miles long, rising from sea level to over 3,700 feet at the Chilkoot Pass at approximately the halfway point. During the winter of 1897–98, thousands of stampeders passed through Dyea and hiked over the trail enduring hardships most of us today can barely envision. Every stampeder was required to pack over a tonne of food and necessities to Lake Bennett and North West Mounted Police enforced this rule at the Canadian boundary at the summit of the pass. The regulation existed for the stampeders' own good since they would otherwise starve or die of exposure. The Mounties were well aware of the situation in Dawson City that winter where earlier arrivals had swelled the population beyond any means of support; there was too little available to support the extra people in the area.

For travelers in 1897–98 there were many amenities along the trail. Of the many camps dotting the route some, such as Finnegan's Point and Pleasant Camp, were simply rest points. In both these places a bridge crossed a creek or river, with a 'modest' toll charged by the builders. Other stopovers were more substantial; Canyon City, a community of log structures almost eight miles into the trail, had been a camp for natives and early prospectors many years before the Klondike Gold Rush and it became a mushrooming settlement complete with freighting services and other businesses. The last major stopover before the final ascent was Sheep Camp formerly used by sheep hunters, over three miles from the summit.

During the winter of 1897–98, when perhaps 20,000 men and women traversed the Chilkoot Trail, the weather often held people captive at Sheep Camp. The population would grow enormously as more prospectors piled in from Dyea during those conditions waiting to assault the summit when the weather cleared. Thus the population of Sheep Camp during the winter of '97–98 is variably reported as anywhere from 1,500 to over 8,000.

There were only two rest points between Sheep Camp and the summit. The first was at Stone House, so named because a large boulder overhung the trail and provided limited shelter.[3] The other was The Scales, at the bottom of the steepest part of the ascent to the summit. Here, packs were reweighed and packers negotiated higher wages for lugging them over this steepest section, where the angle is over 35 degrees.

The men and women who assaulted the Chilkoot Summit were not experienced mountaineers; they were accountants and shop-keepers, cowboys and lawyers, the unemployed and the unem-ployable. Over eight miles of the trail is above the tree line and its steepness prevented the use of pack animals. In the winter 1,200 steps were carved into the ice for the final ascent[4] but, when the snow was gone, the stampeders negotiated boulders the size of buildings. In spring and fall, travelers slipped and slid in the slush and mud. Those who could afford to paid others to pack their goods but most stampeders were not men of means. This, after all, was the reason many of them were on their way to the Klondike. This necessitated their traversing the trail upwards of 30 times hauling their belongings in lots and storing them in caches along the way. It took about three months for the average man to ferry his goods over the Chilkoot Pass.[5]

On April 3, 1898, a tremendous snowslide on the Chilkoot Trail just below the summit buried dozens of people under four hectares of snow. Within 20 minutes, 1,000 men were on the scene digging frantically for survivors. Those not killed instantly by the tons of snow slowly suffocated; their muffled cries for help grow-ing weaker with the passing minutes. The Slide Cemetery is immediately adjacent to the Dyea townsite, bearing silent testimony to the dangers faced by the men and women with gold fever.

Several schemes for tramways were executed during the height of the rush over the Chilkoot Pass, largely in attempts to make the passage through the Chilkoot more attractive than other routes. Early enterprises were replaced in the spring of 1898 by a new aerial tramway, fourteen miles of cable supported by towers anchored in concrete and powered by steam engines at each end. Built by the Chilkoot Railway and Transportation Company the tramway had the largest single span in the world, measuring 2,200 feet between supports.[6]

Beyond the summit, the Chilkoot Trail descends to Lake Bennett, still at an elevation of over 2,000 feet. There the stampeders met up with the people coming over the White Pass and *en masse* they prepared to continue their journey to the Klondike gold fields.

Today the Chilkoot is braved by only a few hundred adventurous souls each year. Interested in experiencing the rigors of the rugged travelers of the gold rush, these contemporary hikers negotiate what has been called the world's longest museum. The trail is littered with relics and artifacts of those heady days of the Klondike Gold Rush. Part of the Klondike Gold Rush National Historic Park, the trail is jointly maintained and administered by Canada through Parks Canada and by the United States through their National Park Service. Hikers are cautioned not to disturb or remove any artifacts and certainly few would consider such an affront to the historical value of the trail but those tempted might be dissuaded by the weight of their packs and rigors of the trail. One wonders how many of today's hikers could carry twice the weight, turn around at the summit and do it again and again and again in the dead of winter.

The dauntless hikers of today have modern advantages over the gold rushers but there are some challenges today that were not an issue a hundred years ago. While today's tents are lightweight nylon, food is dehydrated and no grim-faced Mountie waits at the summit to weigh your pack for your tonne of provisions (however, Canada Customs does have an officer stationed at Fraser, British Columbia who requires a visit from persons arriving in Canada) today your group would be taxed by an event as simple as a sprained ankle. Hikers are expected to register with officials as to their anticipated time on the trail and will be sought out should they not appear at the other end when expected. Search and rescue efforts may take some time, especially in poor weather, so hikers are well-advised to carry extra supplies.

Potentially more dangerous is the chance that a hiker may meet a bear on the trail. Parks Canada posts lists of locations where grizzlies have been sighted or, more ominously, where there have been 'incidents'. The stampeders of the gold rush had the security of numbers; at any time there were hundreds of people in the immediate vicinity to lend aid.

While the spectacle of hundreds of stampeders bent over in a continuous line ascending the Chilkoot Pass is among the most enduring visions of the Klondike Gold Rush, there were many other ways to reach the Klondike. Just a few miles from Dyea on an adjoining inlet of the Lynn Canal another drama was unfolding.

Many stampeders opted to embark from Skagway, Alaska, the Pacific terminus of the White Pass over the mountains. The pass, although farther from the gold fields of the Klondike and not as well marked, was about 1,000 feet lower than the formidable Chilkoot Pass and not nearly as steep. In their eager anticipation to reach the gold fields, many newly-arriving stampeders were anxious to take what they felt must be the quickest route.

In 1887 William Moore, a retired sea captain, built his home near the mouth of the Skagway River where the good captain elected to live out his time in solitude, existing with the wilderness and savoring nature's splendor. Moore's privacy was shattered as the first gold rushers who had decided on the easier White Pass began to arrive on his land in July, 1897. As throngs of people kept arriving it soon became obvious that some semblance of order would be required. By August, a committee was chosen to properly lay out the townsite with Frank Reid as the official town surveyor. Ironically, one of the town's roadways was slated to go right through Moore's cabin and his home was ordered removed. Moore remained in Skagway for a number of years. He fought his eviction through the court system and was eventually nominally compensated. As stampeders intended for the Klondike and the entrepreneurs who would serve them arrived in Skagway, the town began to take shape, going from one cabin to boomtown of several thousand people in one month.[7]

The funds of the would-be prospectors attracted those more interested in mining other men's wallets. Skagway had a well-organized criminal element and at the top of its chain of command was Jefferson Randolph 'Soapy' Smith, the son of a prominent Georgia Baptist family. He crisscrossed the southern U.S. running scams and shady deals and when his luck ran out, so did he. Soapy's unusual name originated from an amateurish trick played out to unsuspecting dupes in Denver. He sold bars of soap to his operatives in the crowd who in turn unwrapped $20 or even $50 bills from the bars, before the mesmerized onlookers. The result was a flurry of business for the chance of purchasing a bar of soap that might contain money. The officer who arrested him could not remember Smith's real name, so he entered the name 'Soapy' on the files, a label Jefferson Randolph Smith carried for the rest of his life.[8]

Skagway, a frontier town, was isolated from the kind of justice normally administered in the rest of the United States. It was there that Soapy saw the opportunity of his life. His charming Georgian accent and the manners of a southern gentleman combined to fool the people of Skagway into regarding him as a man of honor and high standing. He often organized such celebrations as the Fourth of July Parade with himself as the parade marshal. Meanwhile he would bribe, threaten and blackmail his cronies into doing his bidding, all the while distancing himself from their activities to carry on his ruse.

Soapy had the air of a well-to-do philanthropist. Stampeders foolish enough to flash large rolls of money in town quickly caught the attention of Soapy's little 'welcoming committee'. Under the guise of kindred spirits, gang members would escort newcomers into one of Soapy's gambling parlors where fixed die and marked cards were standard equipment. Those who did not gamble could still lose their money in one of the town's bars buying expensive, watered-down drinks. Those who neither gambled nor drank were simply mugged at the earliest opportunity. People who found themselves suddenly broke often turned to the man in town who had the reputation of helping out a bloke down on his luck and Soapy never turned anyone away. His gifts were always generous. These men, thankful for the good fortune of having run into someone as kind as Soapy, wandered off vowing to exercise more caution, only to be rolled again as soon as they passed the next available alley.

Soapy's corruption is best exemplified by the day of the tragic snowslide at the Chilkoot Pass in April, 1898. Feigning themselves as frenzied rescuers, his thugs dug through the snow searching for bodies to rob. Soapy became the self-proclaimed coroner for the tragedy and corpses were deftly relieved of their earthly riches.[9]

Soapy's company did not confine itself to such vulgar displays of crime. One of their less violent felonies was a telegraph office set up in town to relay the lonely travelers messages back home to loved ones. Correspondents could send off a telegraph for a fairly hefty sum, five dollars, (this was, after all, Alaska), with sound assurances that the customer would be notified immediately of any answer. The answer invariably requested that money be wired back at once for an emergency that had just arisen. Only the most observant noticed there were no telegraph lines leaving town.[10]

Soapy's underworld network kept a finger on the pulse of both Skagway and Dyea and their respective passes. This network, however, stopped dead at the Canadian border. To their credit, the officers of the North West Mounted Police were instrumental in keeping Soapy's hoodlums out of Canada. The Mountie's Intelligence sources kept them pretty much on top of the gang's activities in town and on the passes. As well, the idea of hauling a tonne of goods just to cross into Canada filtered out all but the most sincere. Although Dawson City and its environs had its share of miscreants, Soapy Smith and his lackeys were not among them.

Skagway's permanent residents soon began to connect the high rate of criminal activity with their highly-profiled citizen. Although angry and worried about the reputation of the town, they felt powerless to act since Soapy's eyes and ears were everywhere. It was not until word of Skagway's dangerous reputation had reached the outside and a decline in business threatened, that the town's shopkeepers began to take affirmative action.

On the evening of June 8, 1898, a meeting of concerned citizens was called at a warehouse on the dock to discuss their options with armed guards posted outside of the warehouse to ensure the security of the assembly. Shortly after the meeting began, an uncharacteristically inebriated Soapy Smith came down the road demanding entry into the meeting and brandishing a rifle to reinforce his argument. Soapy confronted Frank Reid, the town's engineer, and one of the guards on the dock. An argument ensued, shots rang out from both men's weapons and Soapy dropped to the ground, dead from a bullet through the heart. Reid was shot in the groin and died after several days of agony. Reid received a hero's funeral while Soapy was buried in an unmarked grave in the town cemetery. So despised was Jefferson Randolph Smith that even the officiating minister could not muster an amiable word to say at his funeral: "His remains lie there today cold and still in solitary death, no worthy mourner near his bier, no tears of sorrow shed by his fellow citizens."[11] Not surprisingly, Soapy's gang evaporated very soon after his death.

A small wooden gravestone was erected on Soapy's grave, replaced sometime later by a small marble one. Souvenir hunters for many years chipped away at the stone until it periodically required replacement. An unsung benefactor continued to send a monthly stipend for the upkeep of the grave.

As a route had already existed from Dyea through the Chilkoot Trail prior to the arrival of the gold rushers, so too did a trail exist from Skagway to the White Pass. It fell to one George Brackett to widen and improve the footpath from Skagway. Brackett took on this task with the knowledge that a railway was being promoted for the White Pass Trail so his road would continue as a supply road even after the railway was completed.[12]

Construction on the White Pass and Yukon Route Railway began in May, 1898 and the tracks reached the White Pass summit the following February at great financial and human cost. In August, 1898, a blasting accident buried two workers under a huge 100-ton granite rock. The slab could not be removed unless it was blasted into movable pieces. Doing so would have disturbed the remains of the workers so they remain interred there today remembered by a black wooden cross. *Black Cross Rock* continues to be a site pointed out to today's tourists on the excursion trains, now a memorial to all who died during the construction of the White Pass and Yukon Route Railway.[13]

One of the many tremendous engineering feats accomplished during the construction of the railway was the cantilever (supported only at either end) bridge in 1901, the tallest steel cantilever bridge in the world.

The White Pass and Yukon Route Railway sounded the death knell for Dyea, which boomed in 1897–98. By the following year, anyone with the inclination to go to the Klondike could go through the White Pass in the comfort of a railway car.

Skagway and Dyea, both hubs of seething activity, were similar in many ways. One contrasting feature, however, would have been the population of animals on the streets of the two towns. The White Pass, because it was lower and, more importantly, less steep, was more accessible by pack animals. Less-than-reputable salesmen would often round up wild horses roaming the plains of the midwest and ship them up to Skagway to be sold to unsuspecting customers. Men with no background in handling animals would pay top dollar for a horse that might never have worn a halter, much less been accustomed to carrying loads in a long convoy of man and beast. Any creature capable of having a pack loaded on to its back was pressed into service with the resulting menagerie making for an impromptu zoo of horses, ponies, dogs and mules on the streets of Skagway. The mule's legendary stubbornness made for public displays of temper venting that often entertained the bemused passersby. Panic-stricken horses would also bolt from their new owners, leading them on a wild chase through town. Anyone attempting to stop these rampaging animals did so at their own peril.

Still, a large number of the stampeders obtained animals sufficiently trained or at least subdued to the point where they could be managed. If the burden of the gold rush was physically laborious for the men, it was often a journey of torture and death for the creatures who served them. The tonne of goods per person rule was still enforced by the Mounties on the White Pass, so room in packs was at a premium. Low priority was usually put on the welfare of the animals and precious little fodder was included in the load since many stampeders were under the mistaken impression that grazing was available on the trail and beyond. One source reports that 3,000 horses were taken through the White Pass Trail in the winter of 1897 where most of them died without completing the journey.[14] Another source adds that of the 3,800 pack animals used on the trail in 1897, just 30 survived.[15]

Horses were often left where they dropped; their hapless owners shunting their packs to the side of the trail then hustling back to Skagway to buy another beast. Hikers were obliged to either detour around the carcass or to climb over it. In such situations the dead animal was literally trampled into the ground, its form soon unrecognizable. At approximately nineteen miles into the journey from Skagway the trail traversed a particularly hazardous spot where the path veered close to a precipitous cliff. Here, many of the weakened animals, loaded with heavy and often poorly-balanced cargo, lost their footing, falling to a certain death on the rocks below. So great was the suffering of the animals on the White Pass Trail that some witnesses swore they saw some of the beasts deliberately jump over the edge.[16] This section of the trail was dubbed 'Dead Horse Gulch'; and even the trail became known to many as the *Dead Horse Trail*. The spring floods and run-offs would regularly flush out the decaying carcasses that had collected over the winter and wash them down the Skagway River where they accumulated in town.[17]

The animals that endured the ordeals of the pass and made it to the Canadian border were closely examined by members of the North West Mounted Police. Any animal found obviously suffering or in poor enough condition it could not continue was shot, compeling the stampeder to lug his own load the rest of the way to Lake Bennett or return all the way down the pass for another horse.

Lake Bennett, British Columbia was the beginning of the long water voyage which would take the stampeders to Dawson City. As the rest of the trip was to be covered by boat the voyagers had no further use for their pack animals. The lucky ones were shot and butchered for food. The stingier men, trying to economize on ammunition, released the animals to fend for themselves in a hostile environment ill equipped to support them.

Beasts of burden were not the only animals to travel the passes. A flock of turkeys was transported over the White Pass by some enterprising individuals who already had buyers for them in Dawson at $1.50 per pound.[18] Much to the amusement of his comrades, one fellow brought a crate of kittens over the Chilkoot Trail and made a small fortune selling them to lonely miners starving for company in the gold fields.

Today, the White Pass and Yukon Route Railway continues to operate trains carrying tourists from Skagway through the White Pass and on to Fraser, British Columbia. An antique steam engine pulls the cars away from the station but is replaced within a few miles by a modern diesel engine to handle the steeper grades. The cantilever bridge that was the engineering marvel of 1901 is now bypassed for safety reasons. Brightly colored 'Casey Cars' shuttle hikers between Fraser and the end of the Chilkoot Trail at Lake Bennett.

Although the vast majority of the Klondikers arrived at their goal via the Chilkoot or White passes, there were other routes into Dawson's gold fields. One such approach began at St. Michael, a small village near the mouth of the Yukon River where it empties into the Bering Sea on the west coast of Alaska. From cities on the west coast of North America, travelers were transported by ship up to St. Michael, transferring to one of the sternwheelers plying the Yukon River for a leisurely trip to Dawson City and the Klondike gold fields. This was known as the *Rich Man's Route* because of the phenomenal cost of the trip. Only the more prosperous of the stampeders could afford to pay to be conveyed the entire way to the Klondike. To get as far as St. Michael cost about $1,000,[19] and travelers were still about 1,700 miles from Dawson. Amenities varied widely as well. For some travelers, there was little to do but go out to the deck to get some air, and watch the scenery go by. This trip provided its passengers with spectacular views and stops along the Yukon River afforded the opportunity for short hikes on the river banks. Hunting was sometimes offered from the decks of the sternwheelers and the kill became the main course in the dining room. Once in Dawson, many of these indulged stampeders turned around and went right back home again. For them the point of the whole experience was to simply see what all the excitement was about and having satisfied their curiosity, they boarded the boats for another voyage of luxury back out to St. Michael.

The federal government in Ottawa had become concerned about lost revenue going to Alaskan freighters and outfitters and began to investigate the possibility of an *All-Canadian Route.* They began to promote the Stikine River Trail, which began at Fort Wrangell on the Inside Passage. From there, it traveled up the Stikine River 150 miles, then overland another 150 miles to Teslin Lake north of Whitehorse. The government played up the Stikine Route as one where the stampeders would not have to deal with mountain passes. The route was considerably longer than that through the Chilkoot or White passes and parts of it were nearly impassable but the government promised a railway would be built along the route by September, 1898 and that meant no more tonne of goods to be hauled over inhospitable mountains, no more customs fees on goods crossing into Canada and no more risking life, limb and property in the lawless, unruly American frontier towns of Skagway or Dyea. All looked promising for turning the Klondike Gold Rush into a wholly Canadian party. Sadly, politics intervened and the railway was never built. The bill offering a contract to have the railway built offered the builders a five year monopoly in the area and gave them a four million acre land grant along the proposed rail line. The bill was defeated in the Senate based on the land grant issue.[20] Few stampeders who made it to the Klondike gold fields could truthfully boast they had come by way of the Route.

The federal government was not the only one promoting a Canadian route to cash in on the stampede; before long the people of Edmonton, Alberta began to advertise their town as a starting point for the Klondike. Outfitters sprang up like weeds and packers set up shop. Travelers had the choice of the overland or the water route from Edmonton. Those who chose the overland route had a 1,500 mile hike through barren land ahead of them. Two years' worth of goods would be required to see them through the

26

ordeal. Even those who decided on the water route faced a grueling journey of 2,585 miles that would also take two years.[21]

The editor of Edmonton's *Bulletin* announced that a road with telegraph lines from Edmonton to Dawson would soon be built, hopeful the federal government would come through on his promises.[22] Many benefits were extolled for opting to use Edmonton as the jumping-off point. The most attractive was the claim that one did not need great quantities of food or money; just about $150 to spend on food and supplies as travelers went from one Hudson's Bay Company post to the next on their way to Dawson City. In reality, most of these were long abandoned and the few still in existence had nothing even approaching the quantity of stock needed to service the advancing hordes. In any event, certainly no one could get from Edmonton to the Klondike on $150. Most outfitters offered a years supply of food and equipment for about $300,[23] the assistance of a guide added another $200 to the total.[24] But the trip would take more than one year.

Inspector Routledge of the North West Mounted Police, while on regular patrol in the North, recorded complaints from many stampeders; guides and packers already well into the journey were demanding higher fees, refusing to carry on unless received. Many of these guides were well-versed in the art of haggling from years of dealing with the Hudson's Bay Company.[25]

The natives too had their grievances; the invading stampeders laid waste to much of the land they traversed, fires left burning unleashed havoc and existing trap lines were often plundered and destroyed. Frayed tempers disintegrated into open hostility when the native guides refused to travel on dangerous waterways such as the Liard River, which had been abandoned by the Hudson's Bay Company as a viable route due to its treacherous passages.

The roads leading north from Edmonton dissipated into paths then quickly disappeared, leaving those without guides to their own wits. The soft muskeg sunk the Klondiker's horses up to their bellies and bogged down their wagons. Many repeatedly got lost, wasting time and, more importantly, food. As the precious commodity of fresh food became depleted, the stampeders began to complain of swelling and bleeding in their gums, loose teeth and

27

aching limbs; scurvy was added to their mounting list of problems.

Warnings from travelers experienced in the unique hell of the route north from Edmonton fell on deaf ears in the city. The *Bulletin's* editor rejoiced when he heard some newspapers in the east were singing the praises of the *All-Canadian Route*. Of the estimated 1,500 people who started out on these trails, roughly half of them made it to their destinations; most of the remainder staggered back to Edmonton crippled and half starved. Gathering their dignity, they returned home, some no doubt wondering what had caused this temporary loss of reason.

Those unaccounted for remain between Edmonton and Dawson, interred in the bog. Edmonton continues to celebrate its role in the gold rush with its annual Klondike Days Festival.

The majority of stampeders to the great Klondike Gold Rush traversed the Chilkoot and White passes in the winter of 1897–98. Anxious with anticipation, they waited on the shores of beautiful Lake Bennett for the ice to break up. Some had already experienced the worst of their journey; the trip down the Yukon River would be a pleasant excursion by comparison. For others, their adventure had barely begun.

3

River to Riches

Most stampeders arrived at the headwaters of the Yukon River too late in the season to navigate to the Klondike before freeze-up. A few made the precarious decision to walk the route and risk nature's perils but most chose to wait out the winter on the shores of Lake Bennett where they intended to build the boats that would see them through their journey in the spring.

Today the tranquillity of Lake Bennett in northwestern British Columbia belies the hysteria of the gold rush days. Before the gold rush, Lake Bennett was often visited by Tagish people who hunted and fished[1] but the serenity of the lake was doomed by its geography for it was the beginning of the water highway to the Klondike.

Neighboring Lake Lindemann, also part of the Yukon River's headwaters, is closer to the Chilkoot Pass but the rocky stream connecting it to Lake Bennett is unfit for navigation. Lake Bennett held the best prospects for seeing a boat off safely when the ice broke in the spring yet so many stampeders filed in from the passes in the winter of 1897–98 that the shores could not quarter them all and Lindemann accommodated much of the overload.

The sounds of tree felling, hammering and sawing echoed off the valley walls; the town of Bennett was rapidly taking shape. Banks, stores, hotels and restaurants prospered and several boat-building establishments started up shop. With the local population skyrocketing the boatyards found they could not keep up with the orders. Many stampeders resolved that, if they were to be ready for the first spring breakup, they would have to construct their own conveyance.

Many Klondikers purchased portable folding canvas boats while getting outfitted in the south but apparently transporting these craft over the mountains proved too cumbersome, judging by the quantity littering the Chilkoot Trail to this day.

Unfortunately, many stampeders did not possess the expertise required for the construction of an able vessel and this was where some partnerships began to show signs of erosion. The deficiency of know-how coupled with the inept and definitely unsolicited advice of comrades often generated a heated atmosphere and open hostility regularly blew up at the whipsaw.

Whipsawing lumber was tackled by placing the logs on a tall frame. One person stood on top of the log and his partner stood underneath, manhandling the saw back and forth down the length of the log, cutting it into planks. The partner on top had to maintain his balance and pull the heavy saw upward through the log while the partner on the bottom, had to look up to ensure the cut was staying on line, invariably getting sawdust in his eyes, nose and mouth. This, combined with 'helpful guidance' harangued from the man on top, often finally severed already badly frayed nerves.

It was at such events the North West Mounted Police rendered some of their many services. In addition to their official policing duties, the Mounties were often faced with tasks unconventional but indispensable and the handling and settling of disputes was among their long list of duties. The local North West Mounted

Police officers were often the only ones with whom the would-be scrappers could both agree upon as the arbitrator of their dispute.

Getting the combatants to see reason was not always easy. Often the only way to keep the peace was for the men to divide their assets and go their separate ways. Neither partner wanted to give up a recently completed boat and on more than one occasion an astonished Mountie witnessed the craft being severed in two. Shaking his head as he walked away, the officer no doubt figured that perhaps it was just as well since the destruction of the vessel had probably saved the duo from being drowned later.

The North West Mounted Police served in other ways. The luckless and newly destitute were provided with money. The sick were cared for and arrangements made for the dead. Thieves and rounders were apprehended, tried and sentenced accordingly. A well known anecdote involves an American grifter who was apprehended and detained by Sam Steele at Bennett. Steele reportedly said "Well, seeing as you're an American citizen, I'll be lenient.... I'll confiscate everything and give you half an hour to leave town."[2] Failure to follow Steele's orders which were meant to get boats safely through Miles Canyon brought a $100 fine.[3]

Among the North West Mounted Police's most significant role in the Bennett area was their presence, which helped establish sovereignty. In 1894, the Canadian government sent the North West Mounted Police into the area after receiving complaints that American citizens were taking the law into their own hands.[4] At that time, however, there was little concern for the specifics of the political boundaries since with the advent of the Klondike Gold Rush, Americans in the Bennett area were forming councils and administration committees. When the North West Mounted Police hiked through with supplies to set up customs and border posts at the passes the foreigners were incensed but powerless; the Mounties were equipped with Maxim machine guns.[5] Lakes Bennett and Lindemann were established as Canadian Territory and our American friends were then, as now, welcome visitors. The boundary between the United States and Canada in the Coast Range exists today precisely on the lines established by the North West Mounted Police during the Klondike Gold Rush.

The officer overseeing the policing of Bennett, the passes and the surrounding area was superintendent Samuel Benfield Steele. The personification of the North West Mounted Police, Steele was a native of Simcoe County, Ontario. He was one of the first three men to swear the oath to the North West Mounted Police at Lower Fort Garry, Manitoba.[6] Steele's many and varied experiences and accomplishments had led to a meteoric rise in rank in the force. His achievements included the overseeing and policing of the Canadian Pacific Railway's construction. He supervised the building of the force's new headquarters in Regina (or *Pile o' Bones* as the city was then called) and was the magistrate for the area.[7] It was Steele who introduced the Stetson as the official Mountie headdress, replacing the little pillbox hat.[8] In January, 1898, Steele departed Vancouver for Skagway to assume command of the police in the Bennett area.

The town of Skagway must have been an enormous culture shock for the officer. In his memoirs, Steele recorded the rampant crime; the night air was alive with the cacophony of gun shots, screaming, music, laughing and crying and his cabin was routinely riddled with bullets.[9] Steele administered the police in the Bennett area from the North West Mounted Police office in Skagway (on American soil!) until his headquarters was established at Lake Bennett.

Among the many important innovations Steele introduced was the registering of all boats waiting to depart in spring. This would greatly assist in identifying the missing and dead when the inevitable sinkings occurred along some of the Yukon River's more perilous passages.

On May 29, 1898 Lake Bennett's tenacious crust of ice finally relinquished its grip and, in the next few days, over 7,000 boats set sail from its shores.[10]

Bennett served the stampeders as an important stopover for only two years before becoming a stop on the White Pass and Yukon Route Railway. Few travelers had any reason to stick around, and St. Andrew's Presbyterian Church, built at Bennett in 1899, saved souls for only one season.

The community of Carcross at the opposite end of Lake Bennett, at a narrows connecting it with Nares Lake was originally called Caribou Crossing as caribou were funneled through these

An example of the many hardships endured by the animals of the Rush. This horse is hauling 635 kilograms of gear over the White Pass.

National Archives of Canada/C 20421

The Klondike Highway through the White Pass today.

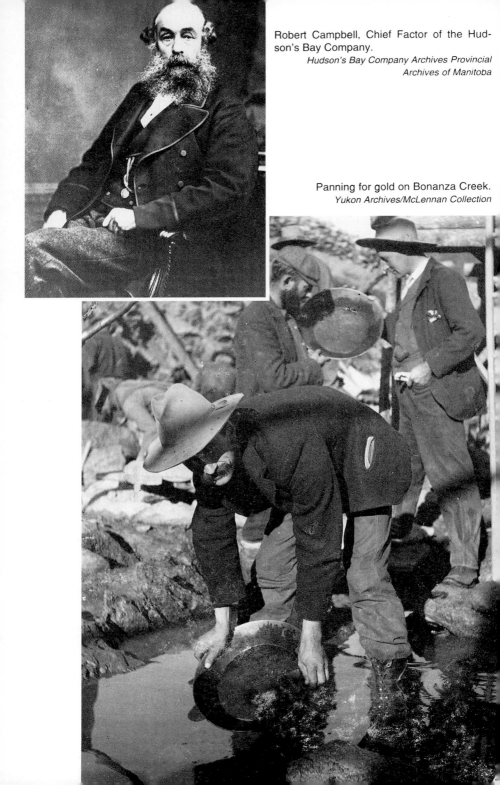

Robert Campbell, Chief Factor of the Hudson's Bay Company.

Hudson's Bay Company Archives Provincial
Archives of Manitoba

Panning for gold on Bonanza Creek.

Yukon Archives/McLennan Collection

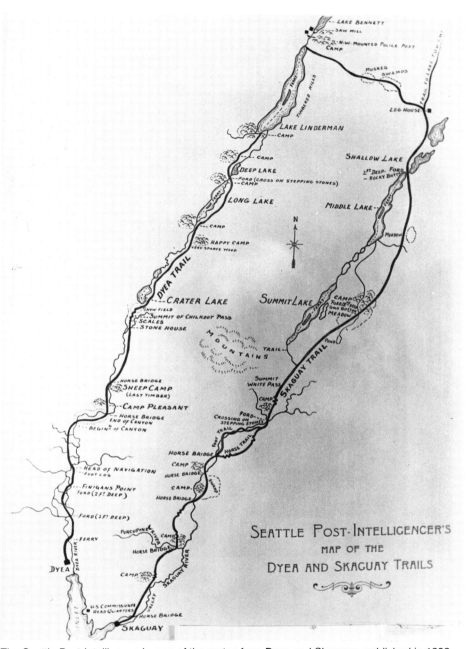

The Seattle Post-Intelligencer's map of the routes from Dyea and Skagway, published in 1898.
Yukon Archives/MacBride Museum Collection

Searchers removing frozen, contorted bodies after the tragic avalanche of April 3, 1898.

Yukon Archives/Atlin Historical Society Collection

The Slide Cemetery as it appears today beside the former Dyea townsite.

Looking up Broadway Street, Skagway, August 16, 1899. *National Archives of Canada/C 28599*

Broadway Street today. Skagway's importance in the Klondike Gold Rush remains evident and the streets teem with tourists during the summer months.

Jefferson "Soapy" Smith, in the wide-brimmed hat and beard, in his saloon, July 4, 1898.

Yukon Archives/National Museum of Canada Collection

The Harper & Ladue Mill Co. office, Dawson City.   *Yukon Archives/MacBride Museum Collection*

An excursion train taking tourists on a trip along the recently completed White Pass and Yukon Route Railway in June, 1900. *Yukon Archives/ H. C. Barley Collection*

Emaciated dogs hauling a ponderous cargo along the Chilkoot Trail near Stone House in 1897. *Yukon Archives/ Winter & Pond Collection*

2.203   A ROCKY LEDGE ON TUNNEL MOUNTAIN.   H.C.B.

An overview of Dyea,
March, 1899.

*Yukon Archives/
Vogee Collection*

Little evidence of Dyea
remains.

The Renton Roadhouse at Minto circa 1900.

Yukon Archives/H. C. Barley Collection

The Montague Roadhouse today. Although these roadhouses are not the same, they still represent a good then-and-now contrast.

Brackett's wagon road under construction in 1897. *Yukon Archives/MacBride Museum Collection*

North West Mounted Police checking stampeders supplies at the White Pass summit, 1899.
Yukon Archives/University of Washington Collection

Sam Steele (North West Mounted Police), shown here on the left, 1899.
RCMP Photo Archives

The *Keno* in 1923.
Yukon Archives/ Hare Collection

Sternwheelers docked at Minto, taking on wood.
Yukon Archives/
Dennett/Telford
Collection

Minto today.

Panorama of Whitehorse, 1900.

Yukon Archives/Vogee Collection

Whitehorse today.

Shooting Miles Canyon, 1898.
Yukon Archives/Vancouver Public Library Collection

Opposite:
A sternwheeler being roped through Fivefinger Rapids.
Yukon Archives/ E. A. Hegg Collection (University of Washington)

The White Horse Rapids, circa 1898.
National Archives of Canada/C 6804

Boat building on Lake Bennett.

All that remains of the wharf at Lake Bennett, B.C.

Canadian Bank of Commerce in Dawson, 1901. *National Archives of Canada/PA 16339*

The Commerce Bank building in 1990, shortly after the bank moved into a new building.

North West Mounted Police Parade at barracks, Dawson, May 24, 1901. Fort Herchmer.
National Archives of Canada/PA 16285

Fort Herchmer today.

49

St. Andrew's Ball in the Palace Grand Theatre, November 30, 1900.

Yukon Archives/Alaska Historical Library Collection

Sternwheelers, including the *Columbian*, at Dawson, 1899.   *National Archives of Canada/PA 16173*

Miners awaiting their turn to register their claim, Dawson, Yukon Territory, 1898.

National Archives of Canada/PA 13413

Third Street looking east from Front, July 1900. This is now King Street.

Yukon Archives/Ernest Brown Collection

A contemporary view of King Street looking east from Front. The restored Palace Grand can be seen down the street to the left, where the banner is strung across the road.

Bird's eye view of Dawson 1902.
National Archives of Canada/C 6366

Bird's eye view of Dawson today.

Top: A group of working girls.
National Archives of Canada/C 14478

William Ogilvie, Esq., Commissioner of
Yukon Territory, 1898 to 1901.
National Archives of Canada/PA 16874

These two pails of vegetables sold in
Dawson for $53.75 September, 1898.
National Archives of Canada/PA 13436

Miners at work during the Klondike Gold Rush.

Sluicing on Discovery claim, 1901.

Front Street looking north, 1899.

Yukon Archives/National Archives of Canada

Front Street looking north, in the 1990s.
Yukon Archives/ Larrs & Duclos Collection

Bowery Street, Dawson, 1898

Bowery Street was the name given by stampeders to this area along the Yukon River inhabited by tent dwellers. Merchants have their wares displayed under canvas awnings.

Yukon Archives/Vancouver Public Library Collection

The waterfront today.

Hydraulicking in the Klondike, circa 1910.

Testing pay dirt samples for gold, 1898–99.

The junction of Hunker Creek and the Klondike River, 1900. *National Archives of Canada/PA 16225*

Antoine residence on Number 3 Eldorado, 1898. *Yukon Archives/Gillis Collection*

Grand Forks in 1903.
National Archives of Canada/PA 16608

One of the few reminders of
Grand Forks.

This building, shown here in 1903, was the Legislative Building while Dawson was the capital of Yukon Territory.

National Archives of Canada/PA 16583

Today, the same building serves as Dawson's museum.

The Chilkoot Pass, seen from the Scales. April, 1899.   *National Archives of Canada/PA 16153*

Belinda Mulroney's temporary tent roadhouse, opened in the fall of 1898.

Yukon Archives/Vancouver Public Library Collections

Joseph Whiteside Boyle, on the left, with "Swiftwater" Bill Gates, circa 1897.

Yukon Archives/Oxford Historical Society Collection

Above: It is here, at Fraser, British Columbia, that today's White Pass and Yukon Route Railway excursion trains terminate their trips through the White Pass and return to Skagway. A Canadian Customs Building straddling the Klondike Highway shares the townsite with this railway shack.

Left: Soapy Smith's grave in the Skagway cemetery.

Below: The Railway operates a small "Casey Car" service from Fraser to Lake Bennett, British Columbia to pick up hikers who have come over the Chilkoot Trail. Here, the cars are pictured at the boarded-up station at Lake Bennett.

narrows during migration. The name was shortened by the author Jack London and *Carcross* became the official name for the town in 1904.[11] Carcross had been a Tagish Indian village prior to the rush where George Carmack's Tagish wife Kate, was born.

The voyage from Carcross was fairly uneventful for about the first fifty miles. The first water hazards were the turbulent Miles Canyon and the frothing White Horse Rapids. The Yukon River raced through the narrow canyon at over twenty-five miles per hour before emptying into the foaming rapids. Those who shot the canyon and rapids and were discharged mostly unscathed after a wild two mile ride considered themselves fortunate indeed. In 1898, five men drowned and 150 boats were lost at Miles Canyon in just the first few days of the season.[12]

At the entrance to the canyon, at a landing later known as Canyon City, the Mounties inspected craft and their pilots for seaworthiness. Steele decreed that women and children would be ordered out of the boats and portaged around the canyon and rapids and, if deemed necessary, a Mountie with boating experience was assigned to pilot the craft. For those who lacked a capable enough boat and/or the visceral caliber to challenge the hazards, a tramway had been constructed through the woods. Established in the summer of 1897, the Canyon and White Horse Rapids Tramway Company made use of horses hauling carts along a double track of logs. Today, traces of the old tramway route remain faintly visible in the quiet woods at the side of Miles Canyon.

The city of Whitehorse at the north end of the tramway, just beyond the rapids, was named after the rapids, but there is some confusion as to how the rapids acquired that moniker. One source contends that a particularly muscular Finn, whom the locals had dubbed the White Horse, drowned in the rapids.[13] Another source asserts that the rapids were named simply because the thrashing waters had the appearance of a rearing white horse.[14]

A powerhouse's dam has since been built to harvest the electrical potential of the canyon and rapids, creating Lake Schwatka and raising the water level in Miles Canyon about fifty feet, taming, at least to some degree, the raging White Horse rapids.

With the hazards of Miles Canyon and Whitehorse Rapids

safely behind them, the stampeders floated downstream into tranquil Lake Laberge, the site of Robert Service's famed story, *The Cremation of Sam McGee.*

Roughly 150 miles downstream from Whitehorse the travelers encountered the Yukon River's next challenge. Five Finger Rapids awaited its turn to thrash the boats to toothpicks. In 1882 W. B. Moore of Tombstone, Arizona came upon four pillars of basalt rising from the river dividing it into five menacing channels. The easternmost channel was safest yet it too exacted a deadly percentage of the stampeder's boats. To take some of the risk out of traversing it, the prospectors devised a winch upstream from the rapids which could ease the craft through the channel and make the passage a little more merciful. For those lucky sailors who survived the watery grasp of the Five Fingers, the remainder of the cruise was an uneventful, if picturesque, 200 mile trip downstream to their golden target—Dawson City.

Dawson City was also accessible from upstream. Steam powered sternwheelers had been plying the North's waterways serving the various outposts and forts since the 1860s. On July 4, 1869 the *Yukon* set sail from St. Michael to become the first steamboat in the Yukon River.

With the increased demand caused by the gold crazed throngs of 1897–98, the boat building facilities along the west coast began a mad race to produce ships. The Moran Shipyard in Seattle boasted a production line that could "build boats by the mile and cut them off where necessary."[15] The design of the sternwheelers had to be such that they could carry large loads (the larger ones handled up to 1,089 tons of cargo),[16] yet still operate in shallow water. The smaller vessels could maneuver in as little as two to three feet of water. "A heavy dew!" as some captains would brag.[17] Due to the physical characteristics nature had bestowed upon the Yukon River, the sternwheelers did not normally exceed 170 feet in length or 35 feet in width.[18] Between June and September, 1898, 57 steamboats landed at Dawson City with over 10,886 tons of supplies.[19]

Depending on weather and traveling conditions, a sternwheeler's boilers could gobble up two cords of wood an hour, necessitating numerous wood camps along the routes. Stops were frequent as the crews trotted up and down the gangplanks with handcarts full of wood.

Small steamers began operating from Bennett to the tramway at Canyon City in 1898. On June 8, 1900 the White Pass and Yukon Route Railway finally pushed through to Whitehorse but there was still a gap in the line from Bennett to Carcross and the steamships *Bailey, Gleaner, Clifford Sifton* and *Reaper* connected that gap in the route.[20] Later that summer however, a bridge constructed at Carcross completed the railroad from Skagway, Alaska to Whitehorse, Yukon.

With the gold rush in full swing the sternwheelers were the link to the outside world. Every ship was met with anticipation and excitement for they delivered food, booze, stampeders, entertainers and, most importantly, news from the outside world. Those already in Dawson City flocked to the river when the whistles from a docking boat announced another load of fresh shipment. The toots of departing vessels trumpeted both the opulence of the fortuitous and the misfortunes of the luckless.

Many hazards lay in wait for the huge fleet. Ice jams and collisions claimed many of the boats and fluctuating water levels and currents created shifting sandbars, taxing the skill of even the best navigators. More bizarre fates also took their toll; the *City of Paris* was rumored to be transporting illicit liquor and was accidentally set aflame by the search party. A crewman aboard the *Columbian* accidentally fired a shot into the vessel's cargo hold that was loaded with explosives, resulting in the loss of six people who perished with the boat. When the *Koyukuk II* was wrecked her engine was salvaged and put into the new *M. L. Washburn*. Apparently the engine carried a curse, for the *M. L. Washburn* sunk at the mouth of the Stewart River in 1920 while on its way to rescue the *Selkirk*; also lost.[21]

By the 1950s, 250 sternwheelers had plied the Yukon and Alaska waterways but sadly, only two remain intact. In Dawson City, the S.S. *Keno* and in Whitehorse, the S.S. *Klondike II* are on display and offer public tours.

The *Klondike II*, built in 1937 by the British Yukon Navigation Company served until 1955 then was given to the government of Canada in 1961. In 1966, twelve persons using three bulldozers and 8 tons of Palmolive Princess soap powder took three weeks to skid the ship through downtown Whitehorse to its present location by the river.[22]

The *Keno* was retired in 1951 after 30 years of service hauling silver, lead and zinc ore. In 1960 the *Keno* made its last run to its final resting place at Dawson, gaining the distinction of being the last sternwheeler to ply the Canadian section of the Yukon River.[23]

Until recently the town of Carcross also boasted a restored sternwheeler, originally built in 1917. The S.S.*Tutshi* was displayed by the Yukon government until it was lost to a fire on July 25, 1990. Some rumors and newspaper reports suggested the *Tutshi* had fallen victim to arson but the Royal Canadian Mounted Police in Carcross now report the cause of the fire as accidental and the case has been closed.

Today the hulking skeletal remains of sternwheelers haunt the Yukon River throughout the territory. Their looming forms slowly disintegrate in the woods near the river's edge or gradually disappear into the sand banks, muted reminders of a busier era.

The frigid arctic winter temperatures closed the Yukon's rivers to the sternwheelers for most of the year. Various companies, vying for lucrative mail and freighting contracts, brought in dogs to haul sleds during the winter. By 1900 the White Pass Railway, which was also running the British Yukon Navigation Company shipping service on the rivers had acquired over 500 dogs for use in the winter. In the summer months, these dogs were cared for on an island in Lake Laberge. A man was hired to stay on Dog Island and look after the animals while they lazed about eating, sleeping and reproducing. Occasionally a steamer dropped by the island to deliver supplies.[24]

By 1902 a winter route, known locally as the *Overland Trail* had been established connecting Dawson City with the White Pass and Yukon Route Railway terminal at Whitehorse. The British Yukon Navigation Company organized a horse drawn stage line service with 250 horses. The trip from Whitehorse to Dawson took five to six days, depending on the weather. Roadhouses dotted the trail, each about one day's travel from the next.

The stampeders cared little what means of transport or route was chosen, hastily selecting whatever was most readily available, least expensive and least troublesome. After all, Dawson City, the city of dreams, land of broken hearts and battered souls, beckoned to them.

4

Destination: Dawson

Stampeders approaching Dawson City in the early summer of 1898 found a boisterous, bustling town where hastily-constructed buildings and tents were dispersed about the townsite. The waterfront, sometimes lined by boats five and six deep, swarmed with newcomers whose bewildered looks of wonder contrasted sharply with the worn and wizened faces of the veterans. All manner of people and animals scurried about the streets adding to the commotion.

In spite of the chaotic nature of early settlement in Dawson City, real estate prices were among the highest in Canada. In the summer of 1897, lot prices in Dawson were as high as $12,000. A year later, choice lots were going for upwards of $40,000.[1] Money really did not have the same value in Dawson City as it did in the south; a single sewing needle cost 50 cents,[2] eggs sometimes sold for as much as $18 per dozen and a can of oysters would have relieved your wallet of $25.[3] Two baskets of tomatoes which would bring a nickel in New York, sold for $5 per pound in Dawson. The Dawson green grocer paid $120 a month rent for his tiny five foot square fruit stall space; in New York, he could have had an apartment for two years for the same money.[4] It has been said that a 25 cent piece was the smallest coin in circulation in the Klondike.[5]

Most new arrivals could not afford real estate so they rented small rooms or stayed in hotels, sometimes working for the owner in lieu of rent while the less well-off shared tents. The fluctuating population of Dawson at this time is difficult to determine since many of the inhabitants were drifters but estimates for the size of the City in 1898 range from 18,000[6] to 30,000.[7]

Dawson's streets were plotted in a basic grid since the townsite was hemmed in on two sides by the Yukon and Klondike rivers and on the other two sides by the surrounding hills. The roads led only part way up the hills until they became too steep to negotiate.

Dawson's swelling population finally spilled across the rivers. In the delta of the Klondike River, where it flowed into the Yukon River, rose Klondike City. Across the Yukon River, West Dawson was established in 1899, in part to isolate its inhabitants from a typhoid epidemic that had ravaged Dawson.

Many entertainers stampeded to the Klondike close on the heels of the gold seekers. In Dawson City, hopeful prospectors rubbed elbows with some high-profile personalities of the time such as Alexander Pantages of the Pantages Theatre Syndicate who had started his career as a bartender in the North.[8]

The Klondike Gold Rush was a dream-come-true for the entrepreneurial at heart. 'Arizona' Charley Meadows and his wife, Mae McKamish Meadows came over the Chilkoot Pass in the winter of 1897–98. Among their possessions packed over the pass were a general store, restaurant and bar. The farther along the trail they went, the more expensive their wares became. Once in Dawson, Meadows constructed the lavish Palace Grand Theatre, using building materials salvaged from wrecked sternwheelers.[9] Meadows was busily getting ready for the first show on the day the theater opened in July, 1899, when he realized seating arrangements had been overlooked. He scrambled around town looking for chairs to beg or borrow resulting in a haphazard collection consisting of stools, kitchen chairs and love seats. It was not orderly but it worked.

The Palace was one of the hottest spots in town, with entertainment ranging from dancing girl reviews to wild west shows to operas. The 'hurdy-gurdy'[10] girls at the Palace made quite a comfortable living; entertainment-starved miners just in from weeks of drudgery in the gold fields were very generous when it came to tossing their nuggets on the stage. Season's tickets for the private boxes in the theater enabled Dawson's elite and their escorts to see and be seen. The boxes were furnished with curtains that could be drawn when the activity going on within was not fit for public viewing.

When the novelty wore off, Meadows sold the Palace Grand. As the theater changed hands, its name was changed to the *Savoy* in 1900, the *Auditorium* in 1901 and the *Nugget Dance Hall* in 1930.[11] Today the Palace Grand has been meticulously restored to its 1899 splendor by Parks Canada, even down to the replica press-back chairs, similar to much of the seating Charley Meadows had hastily collected for his opening night.

Many persons of humble origin made their fame in the North. 'Swiftwater' Bill Gates was one of the lucky ones to make his fortune in the Klondike. Bill was working in Circle City, Alaska, as a dishwasher in 1896 when the news of the big strike in the Klondike hit the area. The next day, Bill reportedly poled a small flat-bottomed boat upstream to Dawson some 275 miles. His boasting about his capabilities with a boat earned him the name 'Swiftwater' from his friends, yet his small arms and paunch suggested that the hard work involved in mastering a boat in such circumstances was not within his area of proficiency. 'Swiftwater' Bill struck it rich on the 'unlucky' Eldorado claim number 13 Above. (For system of numbering claims, see Chapter 5.) His eccentric behavior became legendary: while courting Gussie Lamore, one of the better-known dance-hall girls, he became aware she had been seeing another man. Not to be cuckolded, Bill acted on Gussie's penchant for eggs. One report states that Bill bought up a whole shipment of some 2,200 fresh eggs—the only ones in Dawson—and had them fried up at a local restaurant. One by one, Bill hurled them out the window to the dogs in the street. Another story goes that Bill bought the eggs—at a dollar an egg—and kept them until they were rotten.[12]

Alexander McDonald, the 'King of the Klondike', was probably the richest man of the rush. McDonald hailed from Antigonish, Nova Scotia, and had been fourteen years looking for his fortune in the silver mines of Colorado and a short stint at Juneau, Alaska.[13] Many of the miners spent their gold as fast as it came out of the ground but the 'King' reinvested it by buying more land. In total, he owned and operated over 50 mining properties in the area.[14] He also owned the post office building in Dawson which he rented to the federal government. His holdings increased so rapidly that it was impossible to determine his exact wealth at any time. Eventually McDonald's claims, one by one, were mined out. He died, his fortune much diminished, of a heart attack while chopping wood at his cabin, where he still prospected.[15]

Charley 'Swede' Anderson had been in the Yukon for a number of years prospecting and mining. In Dawson in 1896, while thoroughly intoxicated, the 37 year old 'Swede' paid $800 for a claim that had been considered worthless. In the next morning's painful light of sobriety Anderson begged to have the deal annulled but to no avail. He elected to have a closer look at the claim, which soon yielded $300,000.[15] He was known thereafter until his death in 1939 as 'The Lucky Swede'.

Robert Service has written extensively about the Klondike region and the gold rush and has inspired much of the attention that is now given to that epoch. In truth, however, Service arrived in Dawson City and worked as a clerk in the local Canadian Imperial Bank of Commerce in 1908, long after the rush was over. Today, readings of Service's works are conducted for tourists in front of the cabin where he lived from 1909 to 1912 and where he wrote 'The Trail of Ninety-Eight' and 'Rhymes of a Rolling Stone'.

The Federal government applied a 10 percent tax on all gold leaving the Yukon. Public pressure (mostly American, understandably) demanded a less severe surcharge, so the tax was lowered to 2.5 percent. Gold already formed into jewelry was not taxed so jewelers flourished in the Klondike.[17]

Canadians in the Klondike during the gold rush were far outnumbered by people of other nationalities. It has been claimed that Americans may have comprised up to 75 percent of the total population[18] with the result that many of the social mores of Victorian Canada were not observed. Gaming houses, dance halls and prostitution flourished and several women in the Klondike were involved in one or more of these activities. Estimates of the number of women in Dawson in its hey day range from 1 in 100[19] to 1 in 30.[20] It has been said that, "If men and gold are around in excess quantities, only a certain type of female could handle the resulting mayhem."[21] It is inaccurate and unfair to speak of a common experience among the women in the Klondike, but it is generally agreed that the dance hall girls and their lower class counterparts, the prostitutes, lived a dismal existence. The word *prostitute* was enough to elicit a blush from proper ladies, so such euphemistic names as 'queens of the night', 'soiled doves', or 'lost sisters' were used. Personal stage names were, conversely, quite dysphemistic. There was *Snake Hips Lulu* and the *Texas Filly*. One young woman's upturned nose earned her the unfortunate epithet *Nellie the Pig*. Ethel McNeil was called the *Oregon Mare* for her nasty habit of putting her heavily-shod feet to any unfortunate Klondiker who made the mistake of refusing her a drink.[22]

Hornora Ornstien opted for the more glamorous *Diamond Tooth Gertie*.[23] Her name lives on today at *Diamond Tooth Gertie's Dance Hall* in Dawson City; a must for those who want to sample some of the entertainment of a hundred years ago or try their luck at the gaming tables.

Sam Steele, in Dawson by the summer of 1898, realized the futility of any bid to suppress prostitution; the demand for these services was just too great. Besides, the police were preoccupied with more monumental tasks, their limits stretched by maintaining the security of the bullion passing through their jurisdiction and by otherwise 'Maintaining the Right'. Steele concluded that the best method of both ensuring some semblance of Canadian social values *and* keeping the peace was to sequester the prostitutes to a secluded part of town.

The bordellos were re-established on a small delta in the mouth of the Klondike River. Although officially called Klondike City, this community was commonly called *Lousetown* and was connected with Dawson City 'proper' by a small foot bridge spanning the river. Those traversing this foot bridge were in plain view and the purpose of their destination was never in doubt. The expression 'crossing the bridge' came to be a colloquialism for partaking in the disputable pleasures of all the passion money could buy. So much gold changed hands in Klondike City that several upstarts attempted to stake claims there after finding errant gold dust under the sidewalk planks.[24]

Steele was promoted to the rank of Lieutenant Colonel and assigned the command of the North West Mounted Polices in the Yukon and British Columbia. Steele held various positions in addition to his duties as Police Commander. As chairman of the Health Board he was responsible for cleaning up the filthy sewage conditions in Dawson and requested that Ottawa consult with Siberian authorities as to how they dealt with sewage disposal. Steele chaired the licensing board too and the stringent fees exacted from the saloons and dance halls kept the price of administrating the gold rush from bankrupting the Yukon. Dawson's gambling emporium managers were warned to run a square game, lest a stint at the 'Fort' befall them.[25]

Fort Herchmer, as the police barracks in Dawson were called, was where those sentenced to do time languished. The healthier men were kept busy chopping wood to feed the stoves in the police buildings and other government offices. One imaginative felon exacted his revenge by cutting three months' worth of logs a half inch too big for the standard-sized wood stoves that heated government buildings throughout the city.[26]

Even at the height of gold rush activity, Lieutenant Colonel Steele's time in Dawson was drawing to a close. For reasons of corruption, mismanagement, or just plain overwork, harried and dishonest federal employees alike and their activities were arousing Steele's suspicion. Rumors abounded that the Ministry of the Interior was beset with graft. Concerned for their illicit earnings, government agents in the Yukon successfully appealed to their minister, Clifford Sifton, to have Steele transferred out of the Klondike. The citizens of the Yukon were outraged and numerous petitions and copies of newspaper articles in defense of Steele were dispatched to Prime Minister Laurier, entreating him to reverse the decision. Steele's avowed Toryism did him no favors, for the Liberal leader washed his hands of the issue.[27] In September, 1899 Superintendent Perry relieved Steele of his command and, in an emotional farewell, Steele left the Klondike for the east. Steele's departure was well publicized and documented for few Klondikers were as celebrated as he.

In 1896, the government for the Province of British Columbia was making overtures regarding the annexation of Yukon District but these offers were spurned by Ottawa.[28] The federal government would, no doubt, come to regret that decision, for the managing of the Yukon became an administrative nightmare. The distances alone were formidable; it sometimes took two months for a telegram to reach Ottawa from Dawson City.[29] Almost every issue brought before the legislature seemed a major controversy; policing, liquor licensing, land surveys and gold royalties were just a few of the problem areas and there was the usual bureaucratic bungling. Thomas Fawcett was appointed Gold Commissioner and Land Agent in 1897 and, although Fawcett's honesty and sincerity were never questioned, he was deemed sloppy in the performance of his duties.[30]

Harper's Illustrated edition for the spring of 1898 reported that graft and bribery were epidemic in the governing of the District.[31] Friends of officials could jump line ahead of people who had been waiting to register claims and it was possible to buy information on unregistered claims. On June 13, 1898 Royal assent was given to the Yukon Territory Act and Ottawa was able to rid itself of the mundane day-to-day running of this annoying, yet enthralling little corner of the Dominion.

William Ogilvie, the Dominion Land Surveyor, became the Territory's Commissioner. He had been a member of the team that surveyed the Alaska-Canada boundary and his thorough knowledge of the area made him a fitting choice for the job.

By 1902, Dawson City was incorporated; like the territory it had become too much of an administrative headache to be managed from outside. The rest of the territory was developing sufficiently enough to be drawing attention away from the bright lights of Dawson. Grand Forks, in the gold fields, was also incorporated under the name Bonanza.[32]

Today Dawson City's permanent population is less than 2,000, a fraction of its apex. The sprawling acreage occupied by the immense Dawson City Cemetery offers a poignant reminder of the former size of Dawson City.

Dawson is a service center for the lingering mining industry, but the town derives most of its fame as a tourist attraction. Over 60,000[33] per year visit such attractions as the Palace Grand Theatre, Diamond Tooth Gertie's and the gold fields. Without the tourist trade, Dawson might now be quietly and slowly deteriorating. There are undoubtedly some Yukoners who wish it would be left in peace but instead a restoration program continues to refurbish many gold rush era buildings. To the credit of Parks Canada, the buildings they have undertaken to revitalize have been magnificently and accurately restored. Other structures, like Diamond Tooth Gertie's, are privately managed but are no less lovingly refinished. The handsome old Territorial Legislative building, redundant since the territorial capital was moved to Whitehorse in 1953, has become the town's museum.

The stampede to the Klondike continues today as the curious attempt to experience Dawson's spirit of a hundred years ago. There they see that those who toiled in the saloons and dance halls of Dawson had a life of luxury compared to the men and women in the gold fields. As glamorous and engaging as Dawson City could be, the real action was taking place in the 800 square miles southeast of Dawson City.

5

Pay Dirt

With the Palace Grand Theatre and Dawson's other diversions miles away, the miners labored intently at their claims. Though thousands of men and women toiled in the gold fields southeast of Dawson very few would realize their dreams; most left both broke and brokenhearted.

The Bonanza and Eldorado are not the only creeks in the Klondike. Gold Bottom, Sulphur, Hunker, and Dominion creeks, to name a few, course through the area. It did not take long after Carmack's original discovery for each creek to be occupied from end to end by those involved in harvesting placer gold.

Placer is the only type of gold found in the Klondike. It is collected from the sediment of creeks and streams, having been washed there from another location. The mother lode, origin of the gold, remains as much of a mystery now as it was in the late

1890s. Some contend it no longer exists, eroded away and washed down into the creeks.

Panning was one of the earliest and simplest mining methods. Pans were used to scoop a small amount of sediment from the stream bed and this was swished around in the pan with a small amount of water. Since gold is heavier than the gravel in which it is found the lighter gravel was washed out the sides of the pan leaving behind both gold dust and nuggets. Panning was also a way to determine the value of an area along a creek and deciding whether or not to stake a claim. Ten cents per pan was enough to incite interest in the creek. Discovery claim on Bonanza creek originally produced four dollars to the pan.[1] One of Alexander McDonald's first claims on the Eldorado surrendered $5,000 a day by panning.[2]

Bonanza Creek was staked off by claims, numbered sequentially in both directions from the spot on the creek where gold was first discovered. For example, claim number Three Above was three claims upstream from the discovery claim. Other creeks, such as the Eldorado were numbered upstream from where they flowed into the Bonanza. Each claim was 500 feet long and spanned the creek from bank to bank. Canadian mining law dictated that a person could only stake one claim in a mining district (excepting the discoverer, who could have two.) Thus miners jockeyed for position, wondering whether to stake over here or over there, test panning the creeks and hurriedly running off to see if their pan would yield more elsewhere. It could be a heartbreaking decision; a potential claim left behind in hope of greener pastures was apt to be staked by someone else.

When the creeks of the Klondike were initially staked it was not always with great accuracy. In their frenzy the prospectors could not be relied upon to be precise so, in the winter of 1896–97, the claims were properly surveyed. This resulted in fractions of land between improperly-measured claims becoming available. One such claim was reluctantly staked by Dick Lowe who tried to sell the title to his tiny pie-shaped claim, just twenty-six yards at its widest, for $900. No one was interested, so Lowe worked the claim himself to the tune of $500,000. He had staked some of the wealthiest ground in the Klondike, getting rich in spite of himself. This was Lowe's second fortune. He had first struck gold in the Black Hills and when he lost that fortune, he hit the road trying to strike it rich again.[3] Lowe gradually partied out his new-found fortune; he died in San Fransisco, impoverished, in 1907.[4]

Today the Klondike Visitor's Association owns claim number Six Above on the Bonanza Creek where visitors can try their luck. The rules are carefully laid out on a large sign at the claim. Only hand tools and pans are permitted and camping is prohibited. Of paramount importance is strict adherence to the rules of claim jumping. Any thoughts of panning outside of the claim boundaries are quickly put to rest by these words on the sign: "The boundaries are clearly marked. Do not pass beyond them. Claim jumping is a serious offence."

During the gold rush, the Klondikers were divided into two groups. The Sourdoughs were veterans who had lived through at least one of the area's harsh winter seasons and they often heaped scorn and contempt on the new arrivals who were inexperienced in the ways of the North. These novices were called *Cheechakos*, a Tagish word meaning newcomer. Once the Cheechakos had endured their winter in the North, they too could count themselves among the ranks of the Sourdough.

By the spring and summer of 1897, Cheechakos pouring into the Klondike discovered the creeks had been staked by Sourdoughs already in the area. If they insisted on trying their luck in the gold fields, the Cheechakos could either work claims for other men for salary or a piece of the take or they could pay an extraordinary amount to purchase a claim. There was always the risk the claim was already worked out or had never been worth anything in the first place.

Unproven claims far from the rich creeks, or claims thought to be worth little, went for several hundred dollars. Known rich ground went for several thousand, even for parts of claims. One man, unimpressed with the prospects of his claim staked in the fall of 1896 on Eldorado Creek, sold half of the claim for $800. Later that year, he bought it back for $15,000.[5]

There was another option for the Cheechakos; a few enterprising individuals began to search for gold in the hills overlooking the rich creeks. Newcomer Albert Lancaster found gold in some white gravel in the hillsides but the Sourdoughs continued to ridicule any newcomers, especially those working the hills. Knowing that gold is heavier than gravel, they believed that gold could only be found in the creek beds. What the old-timers failed to realize was that several ancient stream beds dotted the hills.

One Cheechako, Oliver Millet, was puzzled that the gold taken from the Eldorado was of a different texture than that taken from the Bonanza and speculated that the Eldorado had followed a different course in prehistoric times. Millet scoured the hills until he found evidence that the stream bed had once passed to the south of the Bonanza creek. He sank some exploratory shafts and, in his first day of mining, produced over $800 in gold. This streak of white gravel above the creek beds became known as the *White Channel*. Due to poor health, Millet was forced to sell his claim on 'Cheechako Hill' in 1897 for $60,000 and it delivered $500,000 to the new owners.[6] It was not long before mine shafts were penetrating the hills of the Klondike river valley—the Cheechakos had the last laugh.

With the readily-accessible gold harvested and because hand mining was said to be only 25 percent reliable[7] the miners began to use more advanced methods but both panning and the more sophisticated procedures had one common requirement: water.

Sluicing for gold involved a series of tilted boxes with ridges or riffles along the bottom. Gold-laden gravel was loaded into the boxes and, as water washed over the pay dirt, the heavier gold fell into the ridges and the gravel washed away.

In the winter, the frost-hardened ground was melted with fires and later, steam. The softened muck was stored in a pile until spring, when water could be used to sluice out its treasure.

Sluicing could be accomplished only where there was an ample supply of running water. Those mining the *benches*, as the hillside claims were called, had no immediate proximity to running water. The White Channel, for example, was about 100 yards above the Eldorado Creek. The problem was rectified by the construction of the $3,000,000 Yukon Ditch. This aqueduct transported water to the Klondike region from the Twelve Mile River, seventy-five miles away, supplying the bench miners with a capacity of 55,000 gallons of water per minute.[8]

Sometimes the miners used pressurized water cannons, called *monitors,* to loosen the gold-bearing turf, which was then sluiced. This method was called Hydraulic Mining, or *Hydraulicking.*

Many Cheechakos chose not to try their fortunes in the creeks. Those endowed with shrewd business judgment prospered without the necessity of wetting their hands in the freezing streams. One such enterprising celebrity was Belinda Mulroney. Arriving in Dawson in 1897, she had come over the Chilkoot Pass loaded down with merchandise which she swiftly retailed for a 600 percent profit. She built the elegant Fair View Hotel in Dawson City and was instrumental in early housing projects there. Convinced that the miners required services closer to the gold-bearing creeks, Mulroney built the Grand Forks Hotel at the junction of the Bonanza and Eldorado Creeks. The town of Grand Forks would eventually amass a population of 10,000.[9]

Joseph Whiteside Boyle has been revered by many historians as a significant contributor to the Klondike's story, yet he also had a major hand in what became the deterioration of the great Rush mentality. Some descendants of many original gold rushers would maintain that Joe Boyle stole their ancestors' claims.[10]

Boyle, from Woodstock, Ontario, originally came north in 1896 in an attempt to spark some interest in boxing while managing an Australian pugilist named Frank Slavin.[11] With news of the gold finds around Dawson, Boyle and Slavin were off to the Klondike to try their luck.

Not interested in a mere claim or two, Boyle had designs on sizable tracts of land and waterways for large-scale mining. His concerns also included substantial timber rights for he quite astutely realized that, next to gold, lumber was the most valuable resource in the North. The erupting construction industry had an insatiable need for wood and trees grew slowly in the harsh Arctic climate.

Boyle's ambitions required ministerial support from Ottawa so, in February, 1898 he went to Ottawa to petition the Minister of the Interior. On June 11, 1898, the Yukon's Gold Commissioner, Thomas Fawcett received instructions to reserve for Boyle an eight mile stretch of the Klondike River from Hunker Creek to the Bonanza Ferry.[12]

Other miners began to express discontentment over Boyle's successes. Not only were the timber rights being swallowed up, but much of the land that had been used for dumping the waste gravel and dirt from the mining operations was now off limits. Many placer miners lost their claims.[13] The friction was exemplified in some trespassing charges laid by Slavin and Boyle when they caught people stealing wood on their land. Assault charges against Slavin, who had tried to eject the poachers, were contemplated but, in the end, the trespassers were convicted and sentenced to four months of hard labor chopping wood at the Fort. Public outcry over the severity of the sentences was expressed in the local media. A local councillor demanded a pardon for the convicted men.[14]

With larger scale mechanized mining in the Klondike and increases in Boyle's holdings came another of his many enterprises; the mighty dredges. The first of these floating ore-processing factories in the Klondike was built at the Cassiar Bar on the Yukon River in 1899 then transferred to Bonanza Creek. In short order, more dredges were constructed on the gold-rich streams. The dredges crept about, forming their own ponds, digging up the ore with a series of chain-driven buckets. This ore was hauled into the dredge and processed through revolving screen filters and the tailings deposited out the rear. Dredge size was determined by the cubic foot volume of its individual buckets. The smallest dredge in the Klondike employed 2 1/2 cubic foot buckets and the largest dredge used immense sixteen cubic foot buckets weighing 4,600 pounds each. The largest wooden, bucket-line dredge in North America is the electrically-powered (from a plant on the Klondike River) dredge number four which now can be visited on Claim 17 below Discovery on Bonanza Creek.[15] As late as 1957, ten dredges still operated in the Klondike.[16]

As productive as the dredges were they still could not harvest the finest gold powder nor the larger nuggets that were too big for the filter's mesh. Some of the tailings have been re-mined but they still contain unknown quantities of gold the dredges failed to harvest. Tailing piles are a prominent feature of the Klondike

Valley today but roadside signs warn against digging in or climbing up on the piles. Clearly they continue to be of value but whether historically, financially or both is difficult to discern.

Dawson City's newspapers continued to hound Boyle despite his numerous contributions to the community. The transfer of his mining properties to the Canadian Klondyke Mining Company Limited in 1904 did little to shake the determined journalists. They must have considered him fair game because he still held interests as a major stockholder in the company. In 1905 the press still relentlessly denounced him for his conspiracy with Sifton over the extensive timber rights granted to Boyle.[17]

Boyle left the Klondike with his business affairs in disarray. World War One had in part been a cause of spiraling operating expenses and, in 1916, Boyle was having difficulty meeting the payroll of his mining company. Absorbed in the goings-on of the war in Europe, increasingly dissatisfied with the day-to-day running of his mining operations and increased friction with rival mining operations, Boyle left the Yukon forever in 1916.[18]

As early as August, 1899, a scant three years after Carmack's discovery, the tide was starting to turn for Dawson and the Klondike area. Movement of people was no longer one of immigration, but emigration. Several factors precipitated this exodus, not the least of which was the growing number of anxious miners and the diminishing number of available claims and opportunities. In 1898, there were reports of 30,000 persons in Dawson; by 1901 there were only 27,000 people in all of the Yukon, a quarter of them in Dawson.[19] In 1899, 8,000 left the Klondike for Nome, Alaska, following reports of gold strikes. Dawson's media reprimanded the populace, warning of rash repercussions for considering these rumors, but the invectives fell on deaf ears.[20] The dredges were another factor since they could mine many claims with a fraction of the manpower. Many of the Americans in the Yukon were just as happy to go chasing off to Alaska and leave Canada and its prudish Victorian principles behind and many of the Canadians were happy to see them go.

Canadian temperance groups began to take advantage of the declining American influence in the Klondike. Clifford Sifton received objections regarding the vice so familiar in the Yukon. In early 1900, William Ogilvie submitted the following statistics to the Minister: eight gambling houses, 110 gamblers, two dance halls, 42 dancing girls and 49 prostitutes.[21] An example of Sifton's unfamiliarity with the Klondike's distinctive character was found in the direction he sent to Ogilvie to terminate these dubious activities straight away. Ogilvie judiciously resisted; such measures had to be carried out gradually to allow the unique economy and social harmony to adjust. Adjust they did, for the Klondike's communities slowly took on the respectable aura of Canada's more traditional towns.

The gold fields remain scarred by the massive digging and dredging and great expanses of landscape have been dug up and displaced, most of it in the form of the omnipresent tailings sprawling throughout the Klondike. The rest of the missing landscape was removed in the form of the $500,000,000 worth of gold garnered from the Rush,[22] and that when gold was worth about $15 an ounce; today gold is worth 25 times that amount.

A hundred years ago, the hillsides of the Klondike Region rang with the excitement and frenzy of the world's greatest gold rush. In sharp contrast to the renovated and re-enacted Dawson City, a visit to the gold fields today yields only faint traces of their legacy. The ruins of small log buildings are hidden by the new growth forest, slowly re-establishing itself on the quarried countryside. A few dredges sit forlornly rotting into their own sludge ponds, the openings in their great wooden sides often agape in a macabre sneer. The creeks have changed course, seeking their way around tailing piles, still muddied by continued quests for gold.

Most of all, the valleys are quiet. It takes considerable effort to imagine these parts pervaded by prospectors and miners, shoulder to shoulder, gripped with gold fever. Now the valleys would be unrecognizable to the stampeders. The landmarks are gone, the townsites are entombed under tons of tailings and the cries of joy and despair were carried off by the wind a hundred years ago.

Notes

Chapter 1

1. Hamilton, Walter R., *The Yukon Story.* Mitchell Press Ltd., Vancouver, 1964. Page 3
2. Wilson, Clifford, *Campbell of the Yukon.* MacMillan Company of Canada Ltd., Toronto, 1970. Page 63
3. Hamilton, William B., *The Macmillan Book of Canadian Place Names.* MacMillan Company of Canada, Toronto, 1978. Page 309
4. Wilson, Ibid. Page 103
5. Wilson, Ibid. Page 38
6. Canada. Environment Canada, Canada Parks Service. "Gold Mining and the Creeks". Pamphlet, 1989.
7. Berton, Pierre, *Klondike: The Last Great Gold Rush, 1896-1899,* Revised Edition. McClelland and Stewart Limited, Toronto, 1986. Page 40
8. Berton, Ibid. Page 43
9. Berton, Ibid. Page 43
10. Berton, Ibid. Page 46
11. Lung-Martinsen, Ella, *Black Sand and Gold.* Metropolitan Press, Portland, Oregon, 1967. Forward.
12. Berton, Ibid. Page 69
13. Canada. Ministry of the Environment, Parks Canada. "Dawson City Buildings: Dawson City, Yukon Territory". Pamphlet, 1982
14. Rayburn, Alan, "George Dawson, the "Little Giant"", *Canadian Geographic*, Ottawa, March/April 1992. Page 104
15. Berton, Ibid. Page 82
16. Berton, Ibid. Page 90
17. Berton, Ibid. Page 34

Chapter 2

1. Berton, Pierre, *The Klondike Quest: A Photographic Essay, 1897-1899.* McClelland and Stewart Ltd., Toronto, 1983. Page 73
2. U.S. Parks Service notice board at the former Dyea town-site.
3. Berton, Pierre, *Klondike: The Last Great Gold Rush, 1896-1899,* Revised Edition. McClelland and Stewart Limited, Toronto, 1986. Page 243
4. Morgan, Murray, *One Man's Gold Rush: A Klondike Album.* University of Washington Press, Seattle, 1967. Page 42

5. Berton, *Klondike.* Page 244
6. Berton, *Klondike.* Page 247
7. Mayer, Melanie J., *Klondike Women: True Tales of the 1897-1898 Gold Rush.* Swallow Press/Ohio University Press, 1989. Page 111.
8. Minter, Roy, *The White Pass: Gateway to the Klondike.* McClelland and Stewart, Toronto, 1987. Page 107
9. Berton, *Klondike.* Page 259
10. Berton, *Klondike.* Page 153
11. Minter, Ibid. Page 216
12. Minter, Ibid. Page 233
13. Minter, Ibid. Page 226
14. Berton, *Klondike.* Page 142
15. Minter, Ibid. Page 139
16. Berton, *Klondike.* Page 143
17. Mayer, Ibid. Page 138
18. Mayer, Ibid. Page 152
19. Berton, *Klondike.* Page 125
20. Berton, *Klondike.* Page 212
21. MacGregor, J.G, *The Klondike Rush Through Edmonton, 1897-1898.* McClelland and Stewart Limited, Toronto, 1970. Page 31
22. MacGregor, Ibid. Page 29
23. Weir, Joan Sherman, *Back Door to the Klondike.* Boston Mills Press, Erin, 1988. Page 59
24. Mayer, Ibid. Page 35
25. MacGregor, Ibid. Pages 61-62

Chapter 3

1. Yukon Tourism. "Carcross and Area" map and information insert. 1990.
2. Stewart, Robert, *Sam Steele, Lion of the Frontier.* Doubleday Canada Ltd., Toronto, 1979. Page 209
3. Stewart, Ibid. Page 213
4. Steele, Col. S. B., *Forty Years in Canada, Reminiscences of the Great North West.* Dodd, Mead & Company, New York, 1915. Page 288.
5. Stewart, Ibid. Page 201
6. Stewart, Ibid. Page 24
7. Steele, Ibid. Pages 165-167
8. Stewart, Ibid. Page 188
9. Steele, Ibid. Page 297
10. Canada. Parks Canada, and U.S. National Park Service. "Chilkoot Trail; Klondike Gold Rush National Historic Park. Leaflet.
11. Lung-Martinsen, Ella. *Trail to North Star Gold.* Metropolitan Press, Portland, 1969. Page 42
12. Yukon Historical and Museums Association. "Whitehorse Heritage Buildings. A walking Tour of Yukon's Capital" Whitehorse, 1983. Booklet. Page 2.
13. Steele, Ibid. Page 311

14. McLeod, Nancy. "Optimistic Whitehorse, Riding the Crest" *Up Here; Life in Canada's North.* May/June 1988
15. Cronin, Fergus. "The Stern Fate of Yukon Steamboats" *Up Here; Life in Canada's North.* December/January 1987
16. Dobrin, Michael. "A Lifetime on the Yukon" *Up Here; Life in Canada's North.* March/April 1990
17. Cronin, Fergus, Ibid.
18. Canada. Environment Canada, Canadian Parks Service. "S.S. Klondike; National Historic Site" Pamphlet, 1988.
19. Cronin, Fergus, Ibid.
20. Minter, Roy *The White Pass, Gateway to the Klondike.* McClelland and Stewart, Toronto, 1987. Page 344
21. Cronin, Fergus, Ibid.
22. Yukon Historical and Museums Association, "Whitehorse Heritage Buildings. A Walking Tour of Yukon's Capital" Whitehorse, 1983. Booklet. Page 24.
23. Cronin, Fergus, Ibid.
24. Hamilton, Walter. *The Yukon Story.* Mitchell Press Limited, Vancouver, 1964. Page 98

Chapter 4

1. Mayer, Melanie J. *Klondike Women, True Tales of the 1897-1898 Gold Rush.* Swallow Press, Ohio University Press, 1989. Page 200
2. Lung-Martinsen, Ella. *Black Sand & Gold.* Metropolitan Press. Portland, Oregon, 1967. Page 118.
3. Steele, Col. S.B. *Forty Years in Canada, Reminiscences of the Great North-West.* Dodd, Mead & Company, New York, 1915. Page 309.
4. Berton, Pierre. *Klondike: The Last Great Gold Rush, 1896-1899,* Revised Edition. McClelland and Stewart Limited, Toronto, 1986. Page 286.
5. Lung-Martinsen, Ella. *Trail to North Star Gold.* Metropolitan Press, Portland, Oregon, 1969. Page 68.
6. Berton, Pierre, Ibid. Page 290
7. Rodney, William. *Joe Boyle, King of the Klondike.* McGraw-Hill Ryerson Limited, Toronto, 1974. Page 57.
8. Lung-Martinsen, Ella. *Trail to North Star Gold.* Page 79
9. Canada. Environment Canada, Canadian Parks Service. "The Palace Grand Theatre". 1989.
10. A Hurdy-Gurdy is a barrel-shaped organ operated by turning a crank.
11. Lung-Martinsen, Ella. *Trail to North Star Gold.* Page 77.
12. Holloway, Sam. "The Saga of Swiftwater Bill." *The Yukon Reader, Vol 1. #1,* Whitehorse. Page 25
13. Berton, Pierre. Ibid. Page 77
14. Berton, Pierre. Ibid. Page 290.
15. Berton, Pierre. Ibid. Page 399.
16. Taylor, Leonard W. *The Sourdough and the Queen.* Methuen Publications, Toronto. 1983. Pages 36-37.

17. Brennan, T. Ann. *The Real Klondike Kate*. Goose Lane Editions, Fredericton, 1990. Page 137.
18. Morrison, David R., *The Politics of the Yukon Territory, 1898-1909*. University of Toronto Press, Toronto, 1968. Page 4.
19. Holloway, Sam. "Sporting Women of the Klondike." *The Yukon Reader, Vol 1 #3*, Whitehorse. Page 11
20. Backhouse, Francis H. "Women of the Klondike" *The Beaver: Exploring Canada's History* December 1988/January 1989. Page 30.
21. Holloway, Sam, Ibid. Page 29
22. Holloway, Sam, Ibid. Page 15
23. Lung-Martinsen, Ella. *Trail to North Star Gold*. Page 188.
24. Lung-Martinsen, Ella. *Trail to North Star Gold*. Page 170.
25. Stewart, Robert. *Sam Steele, Lion of the Frontier*. Doubleday Canada Limited, Toronto, 1979. Page 222.
26. Stewart, Robert. Ibid. Page 220.
27. Stewart, Robert. Ibid. Page 230.
28. Morrison, David R. Ibid. Page 10.
29. Sawatsky, Don. "Booze made the Yukon What it is Today" *Yukon News*, June 14, 1991.
30. Morrison, David R., Ibid. Page 13.
31. Morrison, David R., Ibid. Page 12.
32. Morrison, David R., Ibid. Page 41.
33. Klondike Visitors Association. Telephone interview. 18 March, 1994.

Chapter 5

1. Berton, Pierre. *Klondike: The Last Great Gold Rush, 1896-1899*, Revised Edition. McClelland and Stewart Limited, Toronto, 1986. Page 43.
2. Berton, Ibid. Page 55
3. Berton, Ibid. Page 73
4. Yukon, historical plaque on site, "Lowe's Fraction"
5. Berton, Ibid. Page 53
6. Yukon, historical plaque on site, "Cheechako Hill"
7. Taylor, Leonard W. *The Sourdough and the Queen*. Methuen Publications, Toronto. 1983. Page 40.
8. Yukon, historical plaque on site, "Yukon Ditch"
9. Sign near townsite. See photo page 60.
10. Whyard, Flo. "The King of the Klondike Comes Home" *Up Here, Life in Canada's North* February/March 1987. Page 65
11. Rodney, William. *Joe Boyle, King of the Klondike*. McGraw-Hill Ryerson Limited, Toronto, 1974. Page 12
12. Rodney, William. Ibid. Page 29.
13. Rodney, William. Ibid. Pages 42-43.
14. Taylor, Leonard. Ibid. Page 68.
15. Canada. Environment Canada. "Gold Dredges". 1984.
16. Hamilton, Walter. *The Yukon Story*. Mitchell Press Limited, Vancouver, 1964. Page 75.

17. Rodney, William. Ibid. Page 63.
18. Rodney, William. Ibid. Page 113.
19. Rodney, William. Ibid. Page 57.
20. Taylor, Leonard. Ibid. Page 59.
21. Morrison, David R., *The Politics of the Yukon Territory, 1898-1909.* University of Toronto Press, Toronto, 1968. Page 39.
22. Canada. Environment Canada, Canadian Parks Service. "Discovery Claim, Bonanza Creek". 1988.

Bibliography

Backhouse, Francis H. "Women of the Klondike" *The Beaver: Exploring Canada's History* December 1988/January 1989.

Berton, Pierre *Klondike: The Last Great Gold Rush, 1896-1899.* Toronto, McClelland and Stewart Ltd., 1972.

—. *The Klondike Quest: A Photographic Essay, 1897-1899.* Toronto, McClelland and Stewart Ltd., 1983.

Brennan, T. Ann *The Real Klondike Kate.* Fredericton: Goose Lane Editions, 1990.

Canada. Environment Canada. *Discovery Claim: Bonanza Creek.* Pamphlet, 1988.

—. *Gold Dredges.* Pamphlet, 1984.

—. *Gold Mining and the Creeks.* Pamphlet, 1989.

—. *The Palace Grand Theatre.* Leaflet, 1989.

—. *S.S. Klondike National Historic Site.* Pamphlet, 1988.

Canada. Parks Canada, and U.S. National Park Service. *Chilkoot Trail: Klondike Gold Rush National Historical Park.* Leaflet, 1985.

Canada. Parks Canada. *Dawson City Buildings: Dawson City, Yukon Territory.* Pamphlet, 1982.

—. *The Dawson City Post Office.* Pamphlet, 1985.

—. *Robert W. Service.* Pamphlet, 1984.

Cronin, Fergus "The Stern Fate of Yukon Steamboats" *Up Here: Life in Canada's North.* December 1986/January 1987.

Dobrin, Michael "A Lifetime on the Yukon" *Up Here: Life in Canada's North* March/April, 1990.

Hamilton, Walter R. *The Yukon Story.* Vancouver: Mitchell Press Ltd., 1964.

Hamilton, William B. *The Macmillan Book of Canadian Place Names.* Toronto: Macmillan Company of Canada, 1978.

Holloway, Sam "The Saga of Swiftwater Bill" *The Yukon Reader Vol.1, No.1* n.d.

—. "Sporting Women of the Klondike" *The Yukon Reader Vol.1, No.3* n.d.

Klondike Visitor's Association, telephone interview. 18 March, 1994, and December 13, 1994.

Lung-Martinsen, Ella *Black Sand and Gold: True Alaska-Yukon Gold-Rush Story.* Portland: Metropolitan Press, 1967.

—. *Trail to North Star Gold: True Story of the Alaska-Klondike Gold Rush.* Portland: Metropolitan Press, 1969.

MacGregor, J.G. *The Klondike Rush Through Edmonton: 1897-1898.* Toronto: McClelland and Stewart Ltd., 1970.

Mayer, Melanie J. *Klondike Women: True Tales of the 1897-1898 Gold Rush.* Swallow Press/Ohio University Press, 1989.

McCready, Marina *Gateway to Gold: Skagway, The White Pass, & The Chilkoot Trail, Past and Present.* Whitehorse, Studio North Limited, 1990.

McLeod, Nancy "Optimistic Whitehorse: Riding the Crest" *Up Here: Life in Canada's North* May/June 1988.

Minter, Roy *The White Pass: Gateway to the Klondike.* Toronto: McClelland and Stewart, 1987.

Morgan, Murray, *One Man's Gold Rush: A Klondike Album.* Seattle: University of Washington Press, 1967.

Morrison, David R. *The Politics of the Yukon Territory, 1898-1909.* Toronto: University of Toronto Press, 1968.

Rayburn, Allan "George Dawson, The "Little Giant"" *Canadian Geographic,* March/April 1992.

Rodney, William *Joe Boyle, King of the Klondike.* Toronto: McGraw-Hill Ryerson Ltd., 1974.

Sawatsky, Don "Booze Made the Yukon what it is Today" *Yukon News* June 14, 1991

Steele, Col. S.B. *Forty Years in Canada: Reminiscences of the Great North-west.* New York: Dodd, Mead & Company, 1915.

Stewart, Robert *Sam Steele: Lion of the Frontier.* Toronto: Doubleday Canada Ltd., 1979.

Taylor, Leonard W. *The Sourdough and the Queen: The Many Lives of Klondike Joe Boyle.* Agincourt, Ontario: Methuen Publications, 1983.

U.S. Parks Service, plaque on site. "Dyea Old and New"

Weir, Joan Sherman *Back Door to the Klondike.* Erin, Boston Mills Press, 1988.

Whyard, Flo "The King of the Klondike Comes Home" *Up Here: Life in Canada's North,* March 1987.

Wilson, Clifford *Campbell of the Yukon.* Toronto: Macmillan of Canada, 1970.

Yukon Tourism, *Carcross Area Map,* with insert. Whitehorse: PR Services, 1990.

Yukon Historical and Museums Association *Whitehorse Heritage Buildings: A Walking Tour of Yukon's Capital* Pamphlet, Whitehorse, 1983.

Yukon, historical plaque on site. "Cheechako Hill"

—. "Lowe's Fraction"

—. "Yukon Ditch"

Index

Classic Adventures

Great Western Train Robberies transports you to the scenes of many of the West's most celebrated adventures. Each authentic episode details the robbery, follows the lawmen through the tracking and investigation, summarizes the notable incidents surrounding the crime, and reports the final outcome. Much of the material, including the many photographs, has never before been released from the railroad files.

Great Western Train Robberies
Don DeNevi
5 1/2 x 8 1/2, SC, 202 pp.
ISBN 0-88839-287-7
12.95

Spring 1995

The Lonesome Lake Trilogy

A trilogy of stories by the Edwards family about their fascinating life in the Bella Coola area.

Ruffles on my Longjohns
Isabel Edwards
5 1/2 x 8 1/2, SC, 297 pp.
ISBN 0-88839-102-1 17.95

Ralph Edwards of Lonesome Lake
Ed Gould
5 1/2 x 8 1/2, SC, 296 pp.
ISBN 0-88839-100-5 12.95

Fogswamp
Living with Swans in the Wilderness
Trudy Turner and Ruth M. McVeigh
5 1/2 x 8 1/2, SC, 255 pp.
ISBN 0-88839-104-8 11.95

Bootlegger's Lady
Ed Sager, Mike Frye
5 1/2 x 8 1/2, SC, 286 pp.
ISBN 0-88839-976-6 9.95

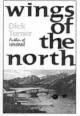

Wings of the North
Dick Turner
5 1/2 x 8 1/2, SC, 288 pp.
ISBN 0-88839-060-2 14.95

Yukon Lady
Hugh Maclean
5 1/2 x 8 1/2, SC, 192 pp.
ISBN 0-88839-186-2 11.95

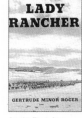

Lady Rancher
Gertrude Minor Roger
5 1/2 x 8 1/2, SC, 184 pp.
ISBN 0-88839-099-8 12

Pioneering Aviation in the West
As told by the pioneers
Lloyd M. Bungey
5 1/2 x 8 1/2, SC, 328 pp.
ISBN 0-88839-271-0 22.95

Puffin Cove:
A Queen Charlotte Islands Odyssey
Neil G. Carey
5 1/2 x 8 1/2, SC, 178 pp.
ISBN 0-88839-216-8 11.95

Yukoners
True Tales of the Yukon
Harry Gordon-Cooper
5 1/2 x 8 1/2, SC, 144 pp.
ISBN 0-88839-232-X 12.95

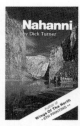

Nahanni
Dick Turner
5 1/2 x 8 1/2, SC, 286 pp.
ISBN 0-88839-028-9 11